Building and Growing
Your Small-Group Ministry

Judith M. Bunyi

DISCIPLESHIP RESOURCES

P.O. BOX 340003 • NASHVILLE, TN 37203-0003
www.discipleshipresources.org

Cover and book design by Joey McNair

Edited by Debra D. Smith and Heidi L. Hewitt

ISBN 0-88177-321-2

Library of Congress Catalog Card No. 00-108419

DR321

Contents

Chapter One
Grounded in Scripture

Pastor Anne Bright attended a conference about small-group ministry. She thought small-group ministry was an interesting concept worth exploring further, so she read about it and discussed it with other pastors. She visited churches that had effective small groups integrated within the life of the congregation. She prayed about it and began to tell members of her congregation about her vision. She did not get far before people began asking her questions about why she wanted to develop a small-group ministry in the church: "Why small groups?" "Why do we need them?" "Why now?" "Why do we have to change the way we are set up?" "Why introduce a new program when we have only a handful of people participating in our existing groups?"

Knowing and being clear, right from the start, about why your church wants to develop a small-group ministry will provide solid grounding for the fire, form, and future of this ministry. Understanding the reasons for having a small-group ministry will help pave the way for answering questions that arise.

The Family

The family, which is the basic unit of society, is the church's primary model for the small group. The Bible is a huge tapestry of family stories. It is through families that God blesses nations (Genesis 12:1-3). Although the Israelites are referred to as "people of God" and "nation," the nation is further broken down into tribes, the twelve subgroups from the sons of Jacob (Genesis 49). Next, tribes are divided into clans (Numbers 26), and clans into families. Scripture

The family is the church's primary model of a small group. Congregational small groups can offer the fellowship, support, and encouragement modeled in a healthy-functioning family.

gives primary importance to teaching about relationships among members of the family and about how they should treat one another. Parents are to teach the laws of God to their children (Deuteronomy 6:4-9; 11:19; Ephesians 6:4), and children are to obey and honor their parents (Exodus 20:12; Deuteronomy 5:16; Proverbs 6:20; Ephesians 6:1-3). Parents need to watch their step, since their children will follow their example. In turn, husbands and wives have Christ's example after which to pattern their relationship (Ephesians 5:21-33).

The moral and spiritual strength of a nation reflects the strength of the families. The dynamics of family relationships play an important role in forming values that will be the building blocks for interpersonal relationships outside the home. As children grow, they see parents and other adults model faith, love, respect, trust, honesty, caring, hospitality, service, stewardship, purity, and other spiritual and moral values. Families are responsible for the care of their members (1 Timothy 5:3-8), and the community is responsible for the care of people who do not have a family (James 1:27).

The family is used as a metaphor for belonging to God's kingdom. A person can have a spiritual family even if he or she does not have a biological family. The Bible teaches that human beings have been adopted into God's family, and that whoever does the will of God is Jesus' brother and sister and mother (Matthew 12:46-50).

Congregational small groups can offer a home in the midst of brokenness. Group members can offer and receive fellowship, support, and encouragement. When group members discuss their spiritual struggles and victories with one another, they grow stronger not only in their faith but also in their trust and appreciation of one another. That is what families and Christian communities are about.

Members of a healthy-functioning family know one another well. Because they live within the same household and are economically interdependent, family members develop more than a casual spiritual and emotional bond. They are able to express and discern one another's needs, which enables them to meet those needs in the most loving, appropriate, and expedient way. The nature and quality of life within the family influences the way they regard people outside their household. Formation of healthy interpersonal attitudes and habits gets its early start within the family. Children first learn from their family attitudes of acceptance and respect, building up of one another, helping and caring, and joy in serving. When adults model these attitudes for children, the attitudes can become the children's lifestyle.

Therefore, it is critical that we, as Christians, attend to the kind of relationships we have within the smallest and most basic unit of society—the family—if we are to model Christ's love in our congregation and in the community. The family and all congregational groups, then, would do well to listen to the scriptural precepts for family relations. How does your family or group measure up?

Jethro's Plan

Exodus 18:13-26 gives an example of the importance of breaking down a large group into smaller, manageable units. Jethro, Moses' father-in-law, observes how Moses is managing the requests for his time and counsel. Jethro believes that Moses' way of listening to each person's case and making decisions about it will wear him out, as well as the people. Sensing that Moses needs to care for his well-being and be more efficient in his problem-solving and decision-making tasks, Jethro proposes a system that will guarantee against burnout. He suggests that Moses choose able and God-fearing leaders to sit as judges. He then advises Moses to divide up the nation into thousands, then hundreds, then fifties, and then tens and to appoint leaders to deal with minor issues. These leaders are to leave only the most important matters for Moses to hear. With this system, more cases can be considered and decided in a shorter time period.

Jethro's suggestion makes sense and seems to be one of the earliest teachings on effective management of time and tasks. A task that is overwhelming can become easier to handle when broken down into smaller steps. With smaller tasks, it is easier to find individuals who can and will do them. The more people use their talents and skills, the easier it is to develop and hone their gifts. It will also facilitate the task of tapping potential leaders for small groups, since the leadership is being shared with them, even if in a limited way. The more people share in the work and responsibilities, the greater the likelihood that they will understand the importance of the task and their role in its completion. If members of the group do what is expected of them, it is also likely that the work will be completed in less time than if one person does the work alone. These are some of the benefits from Jethro's God-inspired plan. What other benefits do you see from following Jethro's suggestion?

Jesus and the Twelve Disciples

Jesus and his original band of twelve followers exemplified the process of learning to be disciples within the context of a small group. He called; they followed. He taught and demonstrated God's love; they watched, listened, and asked questions. He ministered to people; they saw him make the lame walk, the blind see, the deaf hear, and the dead rise. He cast out demons, ate with tax collectors,

Lessons from Jethro's plan (Exodus 18:13-26):
1. Administration and organization require team effort.
2. Delegation of authority yields these positive results:
   - ability to set priorities;
   - ability to tap leaders;
   - more opportunities for instruction, development, growth, and support of leaders;
   - work divided into smaller, more manageable chunks;
   - sharing of responsibilities and stress;
   - more people allowed to participate;
   - more needs met in less time.

> And [Jesus] appointed twelve, whom he also named apostles, to be with him, and to be sent out to proclaim the message, and to have authority to cast out demons.
>
> (Mark 3:14–15)

> And [Jesus] said to them, "Follow me, and I will make you fish for people."
>
> (Matthew 4:19)

> Day by day, as they spent much time together in the temple, they broke bread at home and ate their food with glad and generous hearts.
>
> (Acts 2:46)

> But Saul was ravaging the church by entering house after house.
>
> (Acts 8:3)

talked with outcasts, forgave sinners; they learned from these great teaching moments. Jesus used parables and sermons to teach; the disciples listened, learned, and later asked Jesus about the implications. He slept during a storm at sea; they feared for their lives until he calmed the storm. He agonized in the garden of Gethsemane; they slept. He loved them; they denied him. Together they ate meals, prayed, worshiped, and learned about God. They doubted and believed. They were hands-on disciples, learners and followers of the Great Master and Teacher. Jesus blessed them and gave them authority and power to go in his name. Once they received the anointing of the Holy Spirit, they became leaders who were empowered to tell the good news of Jesus' love. They then challenged believers to lifelong discipleship.

The Gospels give us a glimpse of the teaching and learning process around discipleship. As we study ways of becoming faithful Christian disciples, we can learn from following Jesus' example of teaching his twelve followers to see with their eyes, listen with their ears, and live in close relationship with him and with one another. We can look to Jesus as the author and finisher of our faith, the One who grounds our spiritual being. Following the disciples' example, we can learn to live, laugh, cry, and struggle together. We can learn to care for and to support one another. We can deepen our faith in the company of fellow travelers on the journey to faithful discipleship.

The New Testament Church

The first believers, the New Testament church, worshiped in temples and in homes. They spent time in and depended on both large, public worship and smaller, more intimate circles that met in homes for nurturing their faith and caring for one another. The teachings they received in the temple and in homes were lived out in their daily life with members of their faith community.

The believers "devoted themselves to the apostles' teaching and fellowship, to the breaking of bread and the prayers" (Acts 2:42). "All who believed were together and had all things in common; they would sell their possessions and goods and distribute the proceeds to all, as any had need..., praising God and having the goodwill of all the people" (Acts 2:44-47). "On the first day of the week, when we met to break bread, Paul was holding a discussion with them; since he intended to leave the next day, he continued speaking until midnight" (Acts 20:7).

Teaching and learning were taking place. The apostles explained Jesus' teachings, and people listened in large and small gatherings. They studied God's Word, worshiped, and praised God together. At the same time, they built relationships among themselves through the breaking of bread, sharing of possessions and goods, and fellowship.

Before Saul's encounter with the living God on the road to Damascus, he knew where to find the believers, the followers of the Way, whom he intended to persecute because of their faith in Jesus the Christ. He went from house to house looking for and expecting to find them there. He knew where the church was—in homes. Later, after he himself had become the foremost of Christ's followers, Paul wrote to churches that met in homes. This suggests a continuing tradition among Christian believers of meeting in one another's houses and in smaller circles for spiritual and interpersonal edification. Clearly, spiritual growth, discipleship, mission, evangelism, worship, and service were part of both small and large gatherings.

Paul and His Letters

Paul, in writing to the different churches, hardly mentioned temples and church buildings. His main concern was the spiritual health and well-being of the people who were trying to be faithful in living their new life in Christ. Always of import to him was how they were making progress, from infancy to maturity, in their faith in Christ. He was interested in how they were treating one another after the pattern that Christ had shown them. He wanted to know how the fruits of the Spirit—"love, joy, peace, patience, kindness, generosity, faithfulness, gentleness, and self-control" (Galatians 5:22)—were being manifested in their midst. He named the people he loved and with whom he ministered, one by one, because he knew them well. He had an ongoing relationship with them, even across vast distances. He encouraged them to minister to one another. In Paul's letters to the churches, there are more than fifty "one another" phrases, many of which repeat the phrase "love one another." People and relationships were important to him, just as they are important to Christ.

Throughout the entire New Testament is an unmistakable and overwhelming plea to be mindful of and live out these imperatives in our relationships within and outside our faith community. Scripture commands us to love, serve, encourage, and instruct one another. It teaches us to be hospitable and to exercise humility and equality toward one another. It charges us to bear one another's burdens and to be at peace with one another. Destroying one another should belong to the former things, to our old nature (Titus 3:3). Otherwise, there will be dire consequences (Galatians 5:15). Heeding the call to love one another is, therefore, an act of faithful discipleship and witness to our Lord Jesus Christ.

And every day in the temple and at home they did not cease to teach and proclaim Jesus as the Messiah.
(Acts 5:42)

I did not shrink from doing anything helpful, proclaiming the message to you and teaching you publicly and from house to house.
(Acts 20:20)

Greet also the church in [Prisca and Aquila's] house.
(Romans 16:5)

Give my greetings to the brothers and sisters in Laodicea, and to Nympha and the church in her house.
(Colossians 4:15)

To Philemon our dear friend and coworker, to Apphia our sister, to Archippus our fellow soldier, and to the church in your house...
(Philemon 1–2)

Love one another.
(John 13:34)

Be at peace with one another.
(Mark 9:50)

Welcome one another.
(Romans 15:7)

Bear one another's burdens.
(Galatians 6:2)

Encourage one another.
(1 Thessalonians 4:18)

Serve one another.
(1 Peter 4:10)

Paul also urged the Corinthians to participate regularly in the Lord's Supper, in remembrance of the One who had died for them (1 Corinthians 11:23-26), and to contribute their means to help others in need (1 Corinthians 16:1). He made the following appeal to the Colossians:

> As God's chosen ones, holy and beloved, clothe yourselves with compassion, kindness, humility, meekness, and patience. Bear with one another and, if anyone has a complaint against another, forgive each other... Above all, clothe yourselves with love, which binds everything together in perfect harmony. And let the peace of Christ rule in your hearts... And be thankful. Let the word of Christ dwell in you richly; teach and admonish one another in all wisdom; and with gratitude in your hearts sing psalms, hymns, and spiritual songs to God. And whatever you do, in word or deed, do everything in the name of the Lord Jesus. (Colossians 3:12-17)

Concerning the Ephesians, Paul enlightened them about the purpose of God's gifts and graces and how they were to be used among them. These gifts were given, according to Paul, "to equip the saints for the work of ministry, for building up the body of Christ, until all of us come to the unity of the faith and of the knowledge of the Son of God, to maturity, to the measure of the full stature of Christ" (Ephesians 4:12-13).

As with the first church in Acts, Paul reminded the churches in Colossae and Ephesus who they were and what their mission was. Paul taught them the same manner of living in community as was modeled by the early Christians: Be centered in Christ. Study the Word of God. Teach. Take the sacraments. Contribute to the needs of others. Sing, worship, and pray. Serve one another in love. Almost none of these spiritual disciplines and relational prescriptions can be executed effectively without the presence of others—family, friends, community, and especially those who need love the most.

We can learn about God and about being a Christian. That is the easy part. However, unless we come face to face with the reality, demands, pressures, and expectations in daily exercising our Christian discipleship, everything will be just a futile intellectual exercise. The real challenge comes when we draw together as a community and conflicts and disagreements arise, just as in some of the churches to whom Paul wrote. Yet, when we are able to rise above conflicts and controversies and come together at the Lord's table as one body, experiencing forgiveness from God and one another, we grow in faith.

If we were able to truly identify with the poor, the stranger, and the least among us, we would be living our call faithfully. If the needs of the widows and orphans, the outcast and the hungry, the disposable and disenfranchised decreased significantly or were totally eliminated because we have modeled the biblical prescription for caring and supporting one another, the world would be transformed. If we, who claim to be disciples of Jesus Christ, worked for justice in all areas of life instead of allowing the status quo to rule, peace and righteousness would prevail throughout the land. If we exercised compassion toward our neighbors and attended to the needs of those outside our own parochial boundaries, *shalom* would not remain a dream and a vision. We would be experiencing it right now. These would be the consequences of the transforming power of a Christ-centered life lived out after the scriptural models.

Reclaiming Our Biblical Heritage

When, how, or why we lost the emphasis on small-group life down through the centuries is not important. What is crucial is to realize that Scripture shows us the rules by which we should live in order to connect with God and with one another. It is time we reclaimed the biblical model of worshiping in public and meeting in homes, of gathering in more intimate, face-to-face settings, where we can help one another nurture our faith and follow Christ's teaching to love one another as he has loved us.

We have looked at the biblical pattern of living together in community. We have seen how such a model of bringing our teaching, learning, and practice down to the basic level of the family, house churches, and small groups can promote growth, effectiveness, and efficiency. Indeed, we saw an astounding daily increase in the number of believers, as recorded by the writer of Acts. Perhaps it is not too far-fetched to conclude that this numerical increase was brought about not only by the witness of the disciples' transformed lives but also by their personal invitation for others to taste and see the Lord's goodness.

What is more salient, however, is that our Christian faith, discipleship, worship, service, relationships, and witness are deepened and broadened as we seek to love and serve Jesus Christ and our neighbors, in the power of the Holy Spirit. Spiritual growth and Christian community are not measured by big church buildings and large worship attendance alone. Sometimes they even hinder us from living a balanced life of loving God and neighbor. This happens when we focus on the church as a building, rather than on the church as people. In extreme cases, the brick walls are a testament to the rift among members of the faith community.

We are being called to return to the biblical way of coming to, nurturing, living out, and sharing our faith. Are we up to the task? When we accept the challenge, let us remember God's promise: "I am with you always, to the end of the age" (Matthew 28:20).

Chapter Two
Benefits and Challenges

uman beings are created to be in relationships. We tend to gather, to be together, to form a community, and to be in relationships. Many people think they can go it alone; however, it is the rare individual who can thrive without any help from others. Although conflicts and divisions are inevitable, people stick together for various reasons and for varying lengths of time. Sometimes it takes an extremely unusual circumstance or one of great magnitude to bring people together and to allow the noble human spirit to emerge. In this chapter, we will explore the benefits, as well as the risks, of being in groups, particularly small groups. The advantages and challenges of small groups will be contrasted, for the most part, with larger gatherings.

The list is not exhaustive. Use it as a springboard for discussion as your faith community explores the possibility of building and growing your small-group ministry. Groups will have different insights about the blessings and challenges of small-group life.

Growing Spiritually

Benefits

Throughout history Christians have identified spiritual disciplines or practices that help people grow closer to God. John Wesley often referred to these practices as means of grace. They are ways or means in which people can experience God's grace. While there are many means of grace, Wesley identified these particular ones in his writing: avoiding evil, doing good, participating in public worship,

Practicing the means of grace in small groups helps build and strengthen Christian community as well as individual Christian faith.

praying in private and with the family, fasting, studying the Scriptures, taking Holy Communion, and having Christian conversation.

Practicing the means of grace in small groups helps build and strengthen Christian community as well as individual Christian faith. A synergy and spiritual energy is generated as group members engage one another in faith sharing, intercessory prayer, theological reflection, worship, and fellowship. Members inspire and encourage one another as they attend to the nurture of their spiritual life, individually and corporately. They provide companionship to one another on their Christian faith journey.

In small groups where there are fewer members and more regular gatherings, it is easier for group members to keep focused on Christ and to remind one another of who and whose they are, as well as in whose name they witness and serve. Within the circle, they are able to give and receive support for living as Christian disciples. Help for their faith journey toward becoming more and more like Christ each day is immediate and accessible. Thus, growing from believer to disciple to disciple maker is more likely. Members are given an opportunity to experience spiritual growth, Christian discipleship, and maturity in faith patterned after the example of Jesus Christ and his disciples.

Members of small groups also have plenty of opportunities to be in ministry with one another. They can offer genuine love, hospitality, encouragement, instruction, prayer, and service to one another. This is where exercising humility and equality toward one another, as well as making every effort to be at peace with one another, is put to the test. When members experience peace and harmony, everyone comes out blessed as a result. This also enables individuals to be a blessing to others.

Giving personal testimonies of how we have experienced God in our lives renders meaningful the connection of spiritual disciplines and means of grace to daily life and work. The Scriptures and prayers become more relevant and speak to the day-to-day struggles and victories of participants. Directly witnessing transformation in the lives of people close to us is powerful. We are then assured and become more confident that the grace of God is available to all.

Challenges

It is to the members' advantage to remind themselves of the danger of following the same pattern of activities week in and week out: They might fall into a rut. Doing the same activities in exactly the same manner and order, over and over again, may eventually lead to the loss of meaning of what the group does. The group may study Scripture every week, but nothing should keep them from varying the ways and methods of doing theological reflection on the Scriptures they are studying. God has given people the gift of creativity, so seek the help of the group in keeping your gatherings and activities fresh so that members will always want to come.

Teaching and Learning Together

Benefits

When a group is small, learning needs are easily identified, communicated, and addressed. This, however, also depends on the attitude of the leader and participants. If the leader takes the time to study and find out what the learning needs are, participants are encouraged to identify and express those needs. Thus, searching, developing, or acquiring appropriate learning materials is easier. Learning priorities are more easily determined in a smaller group than in a larger one, and there is more flexibility in setting, format, activities, and materials for teaching and learning. Encouraging and developing an attitude of lifelong learning becomes easier. In contrast to the one-way, teacher-to-participant communication in larger settings, teaching and learning in smaller groups have more impact on individual learners and become more meaningful because of the possibility of increased interaction and multi-directional communication.

Since there are more opportunities to identify teachers, leaders, and facilitators in smaller groups, training and continuing education needs for these people may be provided right away. More one-on-one mentoring can happen. Teachers and leaders may be encouraged to share materials and to tell others about teaching methods, models, and their own experiences in growing as spiritual leaders. They may also be trained and encouraged to develop and produce curriculum materials that are more suited to their particular context and circumstance.

Challenges

Too much flexibility or variety of interests may cause the group to become distracted, thus losing their focus on Jesus Christ and on their growth as Christian disciples. On the other hand, too few members may result in having a limited scope of interest or in staying within their comfort zone all the time, instead of being creative or trying new things. It is useful to have a regular evaluation (quarterly, semiannually, or annually) of your teaching-learning process. It is important for members to keep in mind their mission and purpose for being. Ask, "What is God calling us to do in the area of teaching and learning?"

It is important for members to keep in mind their mission and purpose for being. Ask, "What is God calling us to do in the area of teaching and learning?"

Christian Community: Building Relationships

Benefits

A smaller number of individuals in the group usually translates to greater intimacy among members, based on increased opportunities for interaction, sharing, self-disclosure, and knowing one another. Trust, bonding, and a feeling of community tend to develop at a much faster pace and on a deeper level. With fewer members, the atmosphere in the group tends to be more relaxed and informal. This encourages members to be themselves. Transparency in relationships is the norm, and insincerity is not easily disguised. While accountability seems to be higher, it is usually less threatening in a loving, small group. Because of the informal nature of the relationships, members are encouraged to tell about prayer concerns more spontaneously. Support and help may be provided more immediately as well. Participants learn to be better listeners more quickly. In small groups, the socialization and relational needs of group members are satisfied more fully.

Many individuals feel more comfortable in small groups than in larger gatherings. Those people are more likely to join a small group first, rather than attend a corporate worship service where they do not know anyone. With fewer members in the group, it is easier to notice when someone is missing or hurting and less likely that those who need help will fall through the cracks. Caring for and helping others is facilitated. Moreover, sharing tasks and responsibilities becomes easier; members learn more about a variety of human needs; and interests may not be too diversified and, therefore, may be satisfied more fully.

Other benefits of this category are that group dynamics and processes tend to be less complicated because there are fewer people. For example, in a four-person group, there are six possible dyadic relationships and four triadic relationships. If you increase the number by just two more people, the number of possible dyadic relationships increases to fifteen and triadic relationships to twenty.

Challenges

While some people are comfortable in small, informal settings, others would rather remain incognito. People who are more comfortable in large gatherings will not join groups that are too small.

Some people feel transparent and vulnerable when they are in small groups and, therefore, are less apt to join them. Intimacy and direct accountability, which are more likely in small groups, frighten some people. When a group whose members have developed a strong bond becomes too large, it may be harder to split the group to allow more meaningful relational development.

Group dynamics and processes are sometimes more difficult to handle or manage in smaller configurations. Members of small groups sometimes have difficulty confronting a member because they have grown close to that person. With fewer participants, the ratio of interaction among members will be higher. For instance, members in a four-person group have a larger share of time for participation than those in a six- or eight-person group. While this is good, it also increases the possibility of conflict.

Growing as the Body of Christ

Benefits

If the church is healthy, each small group will manifest that same health and wholeness. Whatever the larger faith community does is reflected in the small-group life. In the same manner, when the small groups in a church are healthy, the church will most likely be robust as well.

Small groups have their place in the life of a congregation. Large gatherings usually provide the setting for preaching, teaching, and corporate worship. Small groups, on the other hand, provide the setting for the faith community to fulfill its primary task of making disciples of Jesus Christ through faith formation, building Christian community, fellowship and caring, faith sharing, accountability, and ministry in daily life.

Small groups may also be the seed for a new congregation. In fact, some faith communities grow out of neighborhood Bible studies and fellowship groups. Because some people feel more comfortable in small groups, it is sometimes easier to invite people who have not had church life experience to come to a small group than to a corporate worship on Sunday. Church growth, particularly in reference to size, sometimes comes as a result of small groups merging with an existing faith community. On the other hand, an existing congregation may use small-group Bible studies as an evangelistic outreach in different locations. In that case, small groups become a venue for the church outreach ministry. Small groups growing and birthing new small groups may be seen as a sign of spiritual growth.

Variety in the nature and ministry focus of small groups will help address a wide range of ministry needs within and outside the faith community. A newcomer or member, then, will have a lot to choose from when determining which group to join.

Challenges

If the church is dysfunctional, each small group also reflects the larger faith community's dysfunction. On the other hand, if the small groups are dysfunctional, the faith community they are part of is most likely dysfunctional as well. In addition, if small groups function independently of the larger faith community, they can be a source of divisiveness, conflict, and perhaps eventual split or demise of the church.

Living and Working Together

Benefits

Groups with a small number of members find a space and a convenient time to gather more easily than large groups do. Similarly, coordinating members' schedules and needs (such as carpooling) becomes less frustrating. The group is more likely to have spontaneous activities and a flexible agenda, time, and format.

As to delegation of tasks, everyone may have work to do. The communication chain is shorter and less complex, so information can reach every person concerned in less time. When there are needs in the community, there are possibly more people responsible for letting church leaders know of those needs. Thus, it is more likely that the group can get the necessary help to the right people in time. Holding training sessions and facilitating group discussions can also be easier because it is easier to coordinate schedules, which enables more people to participate.

With regard to operations, churches do not need huge funds to start a small-group program. Forming and maintaining small groups has a minimal cost, so several groups may be started simultaneously. If more people are involved in small groups, more people can be mobilized for various ministries. For mission and outreach work, the group can determine the kind of project they can manage, physically and financially. It does not have to be costly.

Groups can be formed according to a variety of categories: interest or ministry passion, affinity, age, gender, family, marital status, task, and so forth. A group could possibly exist for every person, if they choose to be involved; therefore, making group life culturally relevant and appropriate is more possible. Forming a new group or restarting/reviving an old one does not require huge funding; however, it does demand a lot of prayer.

Finally, terminating the group will usually affect fewer people and have a less devastating effect on the entire congregation.

Challenges

When there are more tasks and responsibilities than individuals can handle, the group may not finish the task. This is even more conspicuous when there is absence, loss, sickness, irresponsibility, or conflict in the group.

Leader Development

Benefits

Ephesians 4:11-13 says: "The gifts he gave were that some would be apostles, some prophets, some evangelists, some pastors and teachers, to equip the saints for the work of ministry, for building up the body of Christ, until all of us come to the unity of the faith and of the knowledge of the Son of God, to maturity, to the measure of the full stature of Christ." One of the best ways for potential leaders to emerge and develop is to provide them the setting where more-frequent participation is made possible. Small groups, by virtue of having fewer members, can offer more leadership opportunities for each group member—both to discover and to exercise and, therefore, to develop their skills and gifts. Members have more opportunities to try out different things and discover their spiritual and natural gifts. The informal nature and atmosphere of small groups usually provides more room for mistakes.

Small groups also allow more members to use their gifts and graces for the benefit of the whole body and community. They serve as a practical clinic for hands-on training and mentoring of leaders. In smaller configurations, leadership needs are identified, communicated, and addressed more quickly. Thus, the pastor and/or small-group ministry coordinator can concentrate on providing training and continuing education to small-group leaders. Mentoring one-on-one is most likely to happen.

Small groups, by virtue of having fewer members, can offer more leadership opportunities for each group member—both to discover and to exercise and, therefore, to develop their skills and gifts.

Challenges

Depending on the mix of personality types—as well as work, learning, communication, and conflict management styles—the presence of too many dominant personality types may cause other participants to withdraw or decrease their involvement and participation.

People who have less dominant personalities may become dependent on or resentful of the dominant ones. Leaders or members with power and control issues may dissuade potential leaders from performing and participating. They may even cause the group to disband.

Ministry in Daily Life

Benefits

In small groups, it is easier to know who needs what and when. Among themselves, members may develop a process of ensuring timely, efficient, and effective communication and delivery of help. In keeping with Jethro's advice to Moses (Exodus 18:13-26), small groups usually address needs more quickly. The small group may more easily identify problems and issues that are beyond the group's ability to handle and then refer them to others for professional care.

With fewer members, the number of needs is not usually overwhelming. Communication and relationships are less complex, although not totally immune to conflicts. Needs are also more easily expressed, depending on the level of intimacy and trust that has developed among the participants. Intercessory prayers, therefore, not only increase in frequency and quantity but also result in increased member involvement in the care of others. Through small groups, each member is encouraged and given more opportunities for ministry in daily life.

Challenges

Small groups have fewer people to help meet the needs. When confidentiality is broken and trust is betrayed in small groups, depending on the sensitivity of the issue and level of intimacy, there is a higher risk of hurt and pain among those who are affected. It is critical that members honor their covenant of confidentiality.

Fewer people in the group increases the interaction ratio among members, which may be good on the one hand but may result in increased occurrences of conflict, particularly between members with differing personalities or styles of leadership, work, or communication.

Mission and Witness

Benefits

In and through small groups, offering hospitality to newcomers or adding new members is much easier, unless the group is closed. Inviting people to be part of the group will take less effort.

Finding a common passion is more likely than in a large group. Engaging in a mission project as a team can bring members closer to one another.

Members can engage in small-group evangelism, which is less threatening than one-on-one or mass evangelism. However, after gaining experience in doing evangelism in small groups, members may engage in personal evangelism with more confidence. In small groups, members have more opportunities to tell faith stories. Testimonies are more personal and have power to touch lives. Lastly, setting an example for others of how to live in Christian community is a wonderful witness to God's love.

Challenges

A small group may become closed and tightly knit and develop an unwillingness to let in others. If there is already a high level of intimacy among participants, it may become difficult to add new members. In addition, diversity may not be encouraged if the group is formed according to a specific demographic characteristic or passion, such as by age, sex, marital status, race, language, and so forth.

Clearly, there are both benefits and challenges in trying to live out the Christian faith and discipleship within the context of small groups. However, the advantages far outweigh the concerns. By considering both the benefits and challenges, churches will gain an appreciation of the role of small groups in Christian discipleship and be able to plan for the challenges that lie ahead.

Assignment

1. List other benefits of being in small groups as relates to Christian discipleship, spiritual growth, and maturity.
2. List other challenges of being in small groups as relates to Christian discipleship.
3. What other categories can you add?
4. What challenges are unique to your congregation and your small group?
5. How will you use the learning you have gained from reading this chapter?

Chapter Three
Essential Ingredients

Prayer

Why Do We Need to Pray?

sking why we need to pray is like asking why fish need to be in water. Our very existence as Christian disciples is defined by prayer. Prayer helps us connect with the source of power. It is the breath that fills our being and keeps us spiritually alive and dynamic. Without prayer, we will die of spiritual asphyxiation. It is a means by which God's grace flows in and through us. Through prayer, we receive God's blessings and express both our gratitude and our grievance to God. By practicing this spiritual discipline, we flex our spiritual muscles. In prayer, we praise and worship God. We plead and wrestle with God. We intercede for others. We raise our voice of thanksgiving for what God has done for us through Jesus Christ. We ask forgiveness and are forgiven. Through prayer, we seek reconciliation with God and receive the gift of restoration into full relationship with Jesus Christ. When praying, we breathe in the life-giving Holy Spirit that energizes our own spirit and breathe out the love that blesses and enriches our relationship with God and our neighbor. Try praying for someone you do not particularly like and experience how the Holy Spirit transforms you.

What Do We Pray For?

Saturate every activity with prayer. Before you plan anything relating to small-group ministry, get down on your knees in prayer. Pray, pray, and pray, whether you are the pastor, small-group ministry coordinator, or small-group leader. Prayer has no substitute. Ask

Prayer does not stop when you have formed the groups or have started meeting. Prayer needs to be an integral part of the life of individuals and groups, of leaders and members.

for God's wisdom, courage, boldness, and patience. Pray for spiritual discernment in choosing the leaders who will help you in this important ministry, including their training and preparation. Pray for the people who will participate and the gifts and graces they will bring and share in the life of the group. Ask God to help you and your congregation develop your vision for small groups and their role in discipleship, nurture of faith, support, and reaching out to others.

Pray for God's guidance every step of the way. Pray as you make plans. Pray for attitude and openness to this essential and fruitful ministry. Prayer does not stop when you have formed the groups or have started meeting. Prayer needs to be an integral part of the life of individuals and groups, of leaders and members.

As your group meets, members need to pray for those they will invite to the group. The dynamics of your group may sometimes be negative, so everyone needs to spend time praying that God will direct the life of the group. Pray that talents, skills, attitudes, character, communication, and resources will be expressed and shared in appropriate ways among the participants, as well as in ministry and service to those outside the group. Pray for lives that will be touched and transformed through the ministry of the various small groups.

Prayer will also help members discern whether the group needs to continue, make changes, or disband. The interaction among group members, the biblical and theological reflection that takes place within the group, and the support and fellowship that contribute toward building of community will definitely benefit from prayers. Together, group members make decisions, solve problems, and make plans. Earnestly seek God's guidance in these various processes.

If the group needs to choose and use resources and curriculum materials, they need to pray about that also. Pray as you prepare and facilitate the group discussion. Pray for how the studies are going to impact the life of the participants, as well as those with whom they will come in contact.

When the going gets tough, when the life and dynamics of the group appear to be dry and drained, and when your patience as a leader is taxed, prayer will sustain you. In the same manner, when the sailing is smooth and everyone seems to be in harmony with God and one other, prayer will sustain that kind of community life. You have plenty to pray about. Everything and everyone benefits from prayer. In short, praying without ceasing is a requisite for a vital small-group life. If you have not tried it, it is never too late to start. Pray that the presence of the Holy Spirit will wrap around your group and will provide the inspiration and strength to carry on a challenging and rewarding ministry.

How Do We Pray?

You may start praying individually if you believe God has called you to play a significant leadership role in your congregation's small-group ministry. Then, as you start telling others the vision for small-group ministries, invite another person to be your prayer partner. Together, start lifting up specific people who will be open to the vision. Once you have communicated the vision and they have accepted the challenge, form a small band to pray specifically for this ministry, without neglecting to pray individually and in pairs.

If you are the pastor, pray that the congregation will also catch the vision as you talk and preach about the importance of small groups in one's faith journey. Then invite the entire congregation to start bringing it to God in prayer, individually and corporately. You may agree on a time each day (for example, at six in the morning or in the afternoon) to pause from whatever you are doing and pray. Ask leaders of existing groups to form a prayer circle, in order to discern God's will and direction for each of the groups they lead.

Encourage each family to start praying together regularly—for their own family's spiritual growth as a small group and for the evolving small-group ministry within the congregation. Having a family devotional life will impress upon the minds of each family member the importance of this spiritual discipline. When the family prays together for concerns, they are also able to celebrate answered prayers together. When the family struggles together, a stronger bond develops that will support them in their faith journey.

Some people do not want to participate in groups because they are afraid they will be asked to pray. You probably have heard some say, "Don't ask me to pray in public, because I don't know how to pray." In your small group, you may try different ways of praying. You can help people learn how to pray in public by starting with short prayers. These prayers are no less authentic, sincere, and heartfelt than the long ones.

Presence of the Holy Spirit

Prayer and the presence of the Holy Spirit are foundational to a dynamic and transformational small-group ministry. As leaders, we need to recognize that we are not the ones who will convict and transform lives. That is the work of God through the Holy Spirit. What we can do is provide settings through small groups where the Holy Spirit can do its work of transformation. Prayer is our lifeline to the Holy Spirit, who will empower us to do what we were designed to do: love God and love neighbor as we love ourselves.

Encourage each family to start praying together regularly—for their own family's spiritual growth as a small group and for the evolving small-group ministry within the congregation.

If you love me, you will keep my commandments. And I will ask the Father, and he will give you another Advocate, to be with you forever. This is the Spirit of truth, whom the world cannot receive, because it neither sees him nor knows him. You know him, because he abides with you, and he will be in you.

(John 14:15-17)

The Holy Spirit has been promised to us to accompany us on our journey of living as disciples and as disciples making disciples. The Holy Spirit is there to comfort, guide, and encourage us. And when the situation necessitates it, the Spirit is there to empower and make us bold and courageous. However, if we deny its existence and presence in our individual and corporate lives, we stand to lose the power that will enable us to pursue our vision of transformed and transforming lives. It is the Holy Spirit that gives life and meaning to our ministries. Acknowledging that it is God through the Holy Spirit who does the work of transformation is also a sign of humility and acceptance that it is not our might and power that bring about peace, justice, and love to reign in our midst. It is God's work, and we are but God's instruments. Coveting the presence of the Holy Spirit is a sign of our willingness to be vessels to be used by God for whatever purpose God designs. It helps us remember who is in control.

If we insist on controlling everything that happens in small groups, we limit ourselves and erroneously think that the success and effectiveness of our ministry will depend on whether or not we are good. By having the Holy Spirit as our partner in ministry, we stand to gain from the help that comes from God, the Almighty Creator. We need to do our best and give everything we have, but we do not need to carry on our own shoulders the full weight of responsibility for the success of the group.

We deceive ourselves when we think we can do it without the help of the Holy Spirit. We delude ourselves when we forget that real transformation happens when the Holy Spirit is given the freedom to work within the life of individuals and communities. We experience transformation only when we are open to and act on the nudging of the Holy Spirit to be engaged in ministries of justice, forgiveness, and reconciliation. We are transformed and help transform our communities into places where healing and wholeness take place only when the Holy Spirit is given free reign to mold and shape us into the kind of vessel that God can use to bring about peace and harmony. We all need the presence of the Holy Spirit—in the life of the leader, in the small groups, and in the entire congregation.

What Is the Role of the Holy Spirit?

In John 14:15-17, Jesus calls the Holy Spirit "the Spirit of truth," who will be our advocate and helper. In John 16:13-14, Jesus spells out more clearly the role of the Holy Spirit: "When the Spirit of truth comes, he will guide you into all the truth; for he will not speak on his own, but will speak whatever he hears, and he will declare to you the things that are to come. He will glorify me, because he will take what is mine and declare it to you." Thus, if the Spirit of truth is in us, we will be able to discern truth. Moreover, this Spirit of truth has been promised "to be with [us] forever" (John 14:16) and "to the end of the age" (Matthew 28:20). What a glorious and blessed promise. We will not be left orphans. Whether we go through the peaks or the valleys, God will cradle us in the hollow of God's hands through the comforting presence of the Holy Spirit.

When we are preparing to facilitate or participate in Bible study, the Holy Spirit is available to help us discern the truth and how we are going to speak it and appropriate it in our daily life. When seeking direction in our spiritual life, family relationships, work, community involvement, educational plans, ethical choice, choice of leisure or recreation, and all other areas of daily life, the wisdom and guidance of the Holy Spirit are there for the taking. Have you availed of the help that the Holy Spirit offers?

Vision

We can use a travel guide, the Global Positioning System (GPS), or even a simple map to give us a general idea of the direction we are driving. It also shows or identifies the roads, entrances, and exits we need to take to get to our destination. Finding the best route, which does not always mean the shortest, gives us an idea of what to expect. However, we need to keep in mind that we may encounter situations on the road that are not evident on the road map: traffic, road and weather conditions, topography, car repairs, construction, natural disasters, and so forth. Following the directions as closely as possible saves us time, money, effort, and fuel.

If we were to just hop in our car and follow our instincts, we would probably get to our destination by following street signs, directions posted along the highways, and directions from gas station attendants or other people. However, we would probably waste precious time, money, effort, and fuel using the hit-and-miss method.

Building and growing a congregational small-group ministry is the same. If we are not clear why we want to do it, we will just be spinning our wheels. The level of frustration will increase, and the level of tolerance will decrease. Ambiguity of mission, purpose, and objectives will cause confusion and chaos, and heartbreaking experiences will occur more often than heartwarming ones. Group members will miscommunicate, misunderstand, whine, complain, backbite, and argue.

Therefore, it is critical that the majority, if not everyone, be involved in the discernment process for developing the vision and mission of a faith community—from the pastor and key leaders of the church to the youngest member who is old enough to understand what the church should be about. Once the vision has been developed

Assignment

1. Form a small group of individuals with whom you will be in covenant to start praying for God's direction related to your small-group ministry.
2. In the same group, daily seek the presence of the Holy Spirit, in your life and in the life of your congregation. Expect transformation to happen. Find those places where transformation, through the power of the Holy Spirit, is taking place.
3. Plan a church-wide retreat or a retreat for key congregational leaders for the purpose of developing, shaping, or clarifying your vision for transforming and revitalizing your congregation through small groups.

and shaped, it needs to be communicated to every member—through the newsletter, if there is one; pulpit announcements; posters; group discussions; church retreats; committee meetings; all groups, including children, youth, and adults. In short, all people, places, and settings connected to church life. It is the vision and mission that will shape who you are as a Christian disciple, small group, congregation, and community. It is the vision that will generate the passion for fulfilling your mission. Constantly reminding people of your vision, of what you are about as a people called by God, will help unify the congregation toward the goal of loving God and neighbor more strongly and more deeply each day.

I have already expounded on our core mission as Christian disciples and as the body of Christ. It bears repeating that, as Christians, faithfully living the Great Commission and the Great Commandment is a sign of our loving and obedient response to what God has done for us. We are grateful for our salvation through Christ's death on the cross of Calvary and the hope that his resurrection offers.

Within the United Methodist Church, the Great Commission and the Great Commandment are articulated through the primary task of the congregation, as contained in *The Book of Discipline of The United Methodist Church—2000* (¶ 122): (1) proclaiming the gospel, seeking and receiving people into the body of Christ; (2) leading people to commit their lives to God through Jesus Christ; (3) discipling and equipping people in Christian living; and (4) sending people into the world to live as Christian disciples, proclaiming the gospel, seeking and welcoming others into the body of Christ, thus continuing the process of making disciples who make disciples.

For your faith community, you may want to further shape that vision and mission to fit your particular setting, available resources and skills, as well as circumstance. Each small group may also have its own specific mission statement, which is aligned to the overall mission and vision of the congregation. Your mission statement may be in response to the question "What is God calling us to do here (in our community and the world) and now (at this time in history)?"

Chapter Four
Who?

Small-Group Leaders

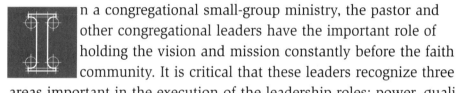

In a congregational small-group ministry, the pastor and other congregational leaders have the important role of holding the vision and mission constantly before the faith community. It is critical that these leaders recognize three areas important in the execution of the leadership roles: power, qualities, and roles.

Power

You have power over me to the extent that I allow you to exert influence on my beliefs, attitudes, and actions. Likewise, I have power over you to the same extent. Though power is sometimes gained by physical prowess or brute force, it does not rely on such factors. In fact, most of the Christian leaders' power depends on sources outside their control, most importantly the Holy Spirit. "But the Advocate, the Holy Spirit, whom the Father will send in my name, will teach you everything, and remind you of all that I have said to you" (John 14:26). When you listen faithfully with your heart, soul, and mind, the Holy Spirit can unleash its power and do its work of teaching and reminding you, of guiding and directing your thoughts and ways. Divine wisdom, courage, and boldness in proclaiming the truth and living your faith are yours to appropriate for nurturing your faith and helping others do the same. When others discern the presence of the Holy Spirit in the leader, and that same Spirit communicates with the Spirit in others, there is power and unity in vision, mission, and relationships.

A second source of power is your knowledge, skills, experience, and qualities as a mature Christian disciple. Other people may allow you to influence them because they perceive you to have some knowledge and expertise that they lack. Be sure you know what your gifts are, but know your limitations as well. Be as objective as you can in assessing your strengths and weaknesses. Do you have a gift for encouraging others? administering? organizing? helping? praying for others? teaching? performing music? Some people are blind to their own gifts. Ask friends to name your gifts, and do the same for them. Observe and listen to feedback from others when you use what you think are your talents and skills. You can discover your gifts by using checklists or inventories. If you know that you are good at something, use it for God's glory. However, you need to know the difference between desire and determination and dispossession. You may desire a talent or ability and have all the determination to acquire it; but if it is obvious that you do not possess a full (or even some) measure of that gift, accept it and focus on improving, refining, and strengthening what you do have.

A third source of power is your role. Being a leader in and of itself adds to the amount of influence you have on others. As a leader, you will assume different roles, and each role may not be equal in the power credited to you. It is important to acknowledge the power, use it wisely, and never abuse it in any way.

Finally, the members of your group are themselves a source of collective power. They may or may not give you permission to hold sway over their minds and passion. Only when they are willing to give you the authority to exercise power over them will you be able to influence them. However, if you compromise biblical principles and moral values so that others may bestow more power on you, it will eventually backfire. When it does, you will also lose your integrity and the power you were coveting.

Qualities

Most of us have met people who have influenced us—for good or for bad. We tend to model our lives after those who have inspired us. But, even at their peak and best, those role models have flaws. However, there is one who stands in our midst as perfect and without flaw—Jesus Christ of Nazareth. "For our sake he made him to be sin who knew no sin, so that in him we might become the righteousness of God" (2 Corinthians 5:21). A pastor or congregational small-group leader is one who patterns his or her life after the Great Leader, Jesus Christ. Pastors and small-group leaders strive to be Christ-like in all their ways: in heart, in thought, in word, and in deed. They model spiritual leadership, servant leadership, shared leadership, prophetic leadership, and accountability.

Small-group leaders model
- **spiritual leadership,**
- **servant leadership,**
- **shared leadership,**
- **prophetic leadership,**
- **accountability.**

Spiritual leadership is the first and foremost quality we seek in those who lead others in Christian discipleship. What does it mean to be a spiritual leader? It is not just something you do or engage in. For example, we may expect a spiritual leader to practice and participate in the means of grace, such as reading and studying the Scriptures, praying, partaking of Holy Communion, Christian conferencing, and so forth. Those are ways that a Christian leader becomes grounded in God through Christ and the Holy Spirit; but if the means of grace are just a list of activities to be checked off, the power of the Holy Spirit does not become evident. Spiritual leaders exude the persona, character, qualities, attitudes, and values of the One after whom they follow and model their life. They have a Christ-likeness about them that comes naturally as a result of being immersed in the relational experience and knowledge of our Savior, Jesus the Christ.

Second, pastors and congregational small-group leaders model servant leadership. They have a servant's heart, are humble, and want to serve others in the name of Christ. Their prime motivation is love for God and neighbor, not their own glory and immortality. As they offer a glass of cool, refreshing water to a tired laborer; wipe the brow of a brother suffering from cancer; offer an arm to the struggling; give bread to the hungry; fight for the rights of the poor and dispossessed; stand up for those abused in any way; and provide safety for children—without demanding fanfare or recognition—we know they have a servant's heart. Servant leaders value others and see them as sisters and brothers who stand in need of God's love and grace. Servant leaders see themselves as channels of that love and grace.

Third, pastors and small-group leaders model shared leadership. If we buy into the idea that leadership equals power and power equals control, it may be hard for us to practice shared leadership. Leaders who are willing to share responsibilities have learned to delegate and empower those around them. They are confident both in their own and in other people's gifts and graces. They help congregational and small-group members discover and share their natural and spiritual gifts for building up the body of Christ. They are not afraid to equip and train others for leadership, which they see as an ever-expanding circle, instead of a limited resource. Those who share leadership have an eye for opportunities, big or small, where others may develop their muscles for serving and leading.

Fourth, pastors and small-group leaders have prophetic leadership. A prophetic leader is one whose heart, mind, soul, and spirit are closely aligned with the will and heart of God. He or she is able to discern God's will and interpret it faithfully to God's people, even if it means risking rejection by the community. We need leaders with integrity who will speak up for justice when called for. We need leaders who will not cower under any pressure or bow in obeisance to any power save that of God. We need pastors and small-group leaders who can serve as spokespersons for God's righteousness and justice, grace and mercy, restoration and healing. Prophetic leaders are imbued with God's courage, strength, steadfastness, and fortitude, as well as God's love, compassion, gentleness, and faithfulness.

Finally, pastors and small-group leaders model accountability. For a long time we seemed to have equated trust with not being accountable or held accountable. When we ask questions, even just for clarification, our motives are questioned. People ask, "Don't you trust the pastor?" We may also be guilty of asking the question, "Don't you trust me?"

It is not that I do not trust you or you do not trust me. However, we have seen and heard of case after case of abuses committed within the walls of the church because no one was being held accountable. Being accountable means being responsible in the way we manage time, talents, treasure, and trust, whether those belong to others or to us. It is stewardship. It is a spiritual discipline. Spiritual leaders need not wait until their integrity is called into question before they begin to be accountable or held accountable. When leaders initiate accountability, both leaders and members are spared hurt and pain, embarrassment, and even devastating legal consequences. That way, we can also see the practice and discipline of accountability as a means of God's grace for all.

In Covenant Discipleship Groups, for example, members give account of how they lived out the terms of their group covenant during the past week. Depending on the specific terms of the covenant, each person tells what he or she has done in loving God and loving others as he or she loves him or herself. I believe that the wrath of God will not fall on us when we fail. However, the process keeps our covenant before us daily, helping us become more intentional in our discipleship. I know because I have experienced it myself. It helps individuals keep striving and growing toward maturity in faith. It is akin to the process of sanctification, of "moving on to perfection," to use John Wesley's language.

When pastors and small-group leaders demonstrate these qualities, others begin to see Christ in them. Jesus Christ was a spiritual leader, a servant leader, an empowering leader, and a prophetic leader who practiced accountability.

Roles

Pastors and small-group leaders play several roles: holder of the vision, spiritual guide, facilitator, mentor, teacher, learner, and encourager.

First, leaders are holder of the vision. The pastor and small-group leader help the body of Christ keep its passion and mission before them constantly. Most importantly, leaders help members keep their focus on Jesus Christ. With vision and corporate life properly centered and anchored in Christ, the congregation, as well as small groups within the congregation, will begin to live their life out of that center. If a congregational group appears to be losing sight of the focus, the leader can use the vision as a compass and steer the group members back on course.

Second, leaders are spiritual guides. Before leaders can exercise this role, they need to be sure that their reservoirs are full and over-flowing. Otherwise, they will be sharing out of nothing. If leaders try to be spiritual guides when they are spiritually emaciated, they may lose their authenticity and integrity. All of us are at different stages in our faith journey. It is possible to learn from even the babes in the faith, just as wisdom and profound thoughts come out of children's lips. However, people expect spiritual guides to be mature in their faith and to have a well of spiritual knowledge and experience from which to draw and share.

Third, leaders are group facilitators, not dictators. From time to time, groups engage in processes such as discernment, decision-making, and problem solving, in addition to building interpersonal relationships among members. As facilitator, the leader guides the members as they negotiate the tricky maze of balancing between accomplishing their purpose and keeping on an even keel the relationships among members who hold varying points of view. It is a tough job, but it is one that a leader cannot afford to ignore if the group is ever to function in a healthy way. The leader as facilitator is able to look at and assess the overall dynamics of the group and to summon all the help, support, strength, courage, and wisdom needed to move toward the group's mission and vision.

Fourth, leaders are mentors, who take others under their wings. Leaders share their learning with, act as coach to, train, supervise, and make referrals for those in the apprentice role. They model behavior and self-discipline for others. They ask questions and offer insights. They challenge and provide constructive feedback at the appropriate time, which is necessary for the mentees' growth and

Small-group leaders are
- **vision holders,**
- **spiritual guides,**
- **facilitators,**
- **mentors,**
- **teachers,**
- **learners,**
- **encouragers.**

development. They guide and give direction, yet know when to let go. They allow those being mentored to be responsible for their own learning and growth. Mentor-leaders are able to keep both tension and balance between telling and delegating, between pointing and empowering. Through this reciprocal teaching-learning process, the mentor and the mentee form a strong bond of relationship.

Fifth, leaders are teachers. This is especially true for those in charge of recruiting, training, and supporting small-group leaders. Providing continuing education is critical. Leaders need to develop an overall plan for education. If they leave it to chance or let it happen in a haphazard way, the ministry will lose its effectiveness. Pastors and leaders who are in charge of training other small-group leaders cannot rest once leaders have been identified. They will need to provide an arena for discussing not only what they are learning in their respective groups but also how they can meet emerging needs. Depending on the preparation of the leaders, trainers may offer either basic, intermediate, or advanced courses on topics they identify as areas of need. These courses may include both processes and practical skills. Pastors and trainers should meet with the small-group leaders regularly (biweekly, monthly, bimonthly, or quarterly) for continuing education, as well as for fellowship and building community. It will help ease the anxiety associated with their role.

Sixth, leaders are learners. They need not only to be open to new learning but also to actively pursue people, places, and opportunities that will help expand their learning horizon. Leaders create settings for learning. They need to be ahead of the game, to be on the cutting edge. Therefore, they should do the following things: Keep their eyes, ears, and minds open to what others are discovering and teaching. Observe, listen, and reflect on their experiences. Mull over and test new ideas and revisit old ones. See where connections are being made. Discuss with others and try to understand where they are coming from. Do their own exploring. Experiment. Read. Ask questions. Compare notes. Weigh options. Take risks.

Last, but not least, leaders become shepherds (encouragers). Shepherds lead the sheep to green pastures, cool water, and a place to rest. When small-group leaders are hungry for encouragement and prayer, pastors and leaders provide that. When they are thirsty for understanding and compassion, pastors and leaders offer that. When they need a break and respite from their cares and concerns, the shepherd gives them rest. The important thing is for the small-group leaders to have a safe place to be fed and supported, to be encouraged and lifted up, to be healed and restored, to offer and receive forgiveness, and to know that they are accepted for who they are: God's children. The shepherds also need to lead so that others will come to know and rest in the love of the Great Shepherd, Jesus Christ.

Small-Group Members

It is essential that leaders of small groups *know* and *know about* the members of their groups. Begin with the obvious demographic data, but do not stop there. It is a human predilection to have certain stereotypes and prejudices about other people. If other group members come from the same racial, political, economic, or religious background, we make assumptions of congruence. Consequently, we might presume that, since they look like us and believe the same things we do, their entire being is aligned with everything we think, feel, and know. On the other hand, if someone is different in color, physical features, language usage, religious affiliation, educational attainment, we make assumptions of incongruence. We presume that, because they appear to be different on the surface, they do not hold the same views or are motivated by a different set of values.

Nothing can be further from the truth. A healthy approach, which encourages building trust and relationships, is to question and test our own assumptions, stereotypes, and prejudices as we get to know others better. Instead of being dogmatic about our views, we should be prepared to be surprised by what others bring to the table. By asking questions and practicing attentive listening, we can grow closer through a better understanding and appreciation of one another.

What motivates the members of your groups? What drives them to behave in a certain way? What is behind their actions? When someone is reticent during group meetings but quite animated when interacting one-on-one, what makes him or her behave differently? A person who is consistently upbeat and positive may be confronted with a different challenge in life than one who is sad, pessimistic, or depressed. However, we need to remember that things are not always what they seem. An eternal optimist, for example, may be using his or her optimism to cover up an insecurity or frailty, while a person going through depression may need time to work through some grief or loss. It is crucial to engage others in conversation and theological reflection, to do some projects with them, or to spend some leisure time with them, in order to see them up close in varied settings. You will be able to read more accurately whether there is an observable, consistent pattern in their outlook, insights, values, and demeanor. The more you build trust in one another, the easier it

What characterizes the members of your small group? How do you see them? How do they see themselves?

What motivates the members of your small group? Where do their passions lie? Why do they do what they do?

is to take your conversations to a higher level of intimacy that allows deeper probing for your and their motivation and passion in life, in relationships, in faith matters, as well as in other dimensions of individual and community life.

Spiritual Needs

A congregational small group gives members a place to seek God in the company of fellow travelers on a spiritual journey. The lives and testimonies of co-sojourners in Christian discipleship can be a source of inspiration to others. The intimacy that the small group offers facilitates sharing life's doubts, victories, struggles, hurts, joys, ambiguities, miracles, and blessings on a more personal level that is not as easily done in larger gatherings.

The practice of spiritual disciplines in a small-group setting may enhance the way members practice them in their individual faith walk. Individuals in the group may influence the depth and extent of how spiritual needs of others are met, when they tell how God is working in and through their lives. Thus, interdependence is created through the reciprocal sharing and meeting of spiritual needs among congregational small-group participants. This, in turn, builds Christian community.

Gifts of Group Members

One of the benefits of being in a small group is that the gifts and talents of each member are more readily recognized than in a larger, corporate setting. Members interact on a more frequent and personal basis, enabling them to know one another's strengths and weaknesses. If several individuals have a gift for leading worship and music, they do not have to wait to use their gifts during large congregational worship gatherings. Those group members may use their talents in the small group during worship. If you have a gift for encouragement, know that you can bless a lot of lives through verbal and nonverbal affirmations. Many people need encouragement, in whatever form: letters, cards, words of appreciation, prayers, flowers, food, or any act of kindness and thoughtfulness.

When sharing responsibilities in your small group, think of dividing the work into smaller chunks. Someone can call members to remind them of the meeting. Another can prepare the refreshments. Someone else can open his or her home for the gathering. While the leader prepares and facilitates the meetings and Scripture study, another member may offer to clean up after the fellowship or lead in prayer or singing. You can rotate the responsibilities among the members. Plenty of work needs be done, and no one person needs to do all the work and suffer burnout as a result. Besides, it is

What are the spiritual needs of the participants? How are they being met?

What gifts do members bring to the group? How are those gifts developed, encouraged, affirmed, and used?

more fun, takes less time to complete the task, involves everyone, and lightens the load when all share in the task. This is also another way of building community and relationships. Think of how you are using the gifts that abound in your circle.

Group Goals

As you define your goals within the context of your particular Christian community, ask yourselves whether those goals are aligned with the mission of the church to make disciples of Jesus Christ. As you seek to know and love God and neighbor more deeply, examine your goals and purposes, as well as the manner in which you strive to attain them. Are they consistent with scriptural principles? Do they help you to be Christ-like in your daily life? Do they encourage you to manifest the fruits of the Spirit and exercise the gifts of the Spirit? Both what the group does and how it does it make an important witness.

Our lives are a constant witness to those around us—our families, neighbors, business contacts, work colleagues, social and professional networks, and every person we interact with on a day-to-day basis. Whether we like it or not, people observe us and make judgments about our authenticity and integrity. They notice something unique when members all try to live out of a Christ-centered life. They know when they see the love of God expressed and demonstrated in the way members relate to others within and outside the group. Do you respect and honor one another? Are you willing to serve one another, or are you expecting to be served all the time? Do you practice attentive listening when someone else has the floor? Do you possess an attitude of gratitude? Are you open and sensitive to the needs of others? In short, what are the norms that rule and guide your relationships and life as a faith community? Do they bear Christ's mark?

Forming Christian Community

One of the goals of encouraging members to be part of congregational small groups is to build Christian community. Humans are created to be in relationships, with God and one another. If the group keeps a balance between these two emphases, both relationships stand to benefit. The corporate practice of spiritual disciplines, as well as total group involvement in outreach and mission projects, builds community. For example, prayer is one way we get close to the heart of God. Intercessory prayer, praying for others and their needs, is an act of drawing close to God. We come to God to express our care and concern for others. That form of prayer meets needs both to be in relationship with God and to be in community with

What are your goals as a group? How are those goals attained?

What norms guide your behavior? How do they support you in living as Christian disciples?

How are you building community? How are you building trust?

fellow Christians. Our common concern brings us closer to one another. Other expressions of caring come in the form of offering and providing support in times of loss and death, sickness, loneliness and separation from family, disaster, need for childcare, and so forth. These acts of kindness form the foundation of a strong community.

Times of fellowship, recreation, and celebration of blessings and victories over challenges draw a community together as well. Laughter, relaxation, joy, and peace strengthen the bond that holds members together.

Trust is built over time. When members tell about their hurts and concerns and the group prays for them, everyone needs to honor the confidential nature of what was told. What is discussed in the group must stay within the group. If members form a beeline to the telephone immediately after the gathering to tell others what they heard, you can be sure that people will feel violated, wounded, betrayed, and even traumatized. This will certainly result in loss of trust, which is difficult to repair and restore. Often, groups that have gone through this disband and disintegrate almost immediately. Moreover, the pain of betrayal seems to haunt and linger for many years. People tend to have a long memory for such experiences. Those who have been burned by it become cautious about disclosing anything in the future. The lesson to be learned is to honor confidentiality and respect the privacy of members.

Individual Differences

Individuals who make up the group come in varied sizes, shapes, and colors. The difference may be in styles of learning, communication, conflict resolution, decision-making, and problem solving, as well as personality types and the way they have been raised. Various groups have their share of the different character types and challenging people: indecisive, emotional, gentle, soft-spoken, fast-talker, peacemaker, smart aleck, intelligent, and many more. Differences in religious traditions or cultural, educational, socio-economic, or political background may affect group participation. Groups may also have differences in gender and generation. In other words, several factors can influence the nature, direction, quality, and extent of participation within the group. On top of these personal factors, physical, emotional, and environmental influences may contribute to the strengthening or weakening of interpersonal relationships.

Sometimes it is inevitable that differences spur misunderstanding and conflict. However, in the context of Christian community, differences can be an energizer and a wonderful source of creativity. The different points of view, experiences, skills, and knowledge can enhance learning and appreciation of others. Members may hear

What factors affect participation in your group? How do those factors facilitate or impede your spiritual growth and life as Christian disciples?

insights and ideas that trigger other insights and ideas. An accepting atmosphere opens the door for telling of personal faith stories, thus inspiring and encouraging those who need to hear them. Those hearing stories of how others have struggled with faith issues and doubts may find strength and courage for their own faith journeys. That is the beauty of traveling side by side with others in the faith journey. That is what is exciting about being a part of a small congregational group.

Assignment

As a group or team do the following:

1. Pray for your pastor and other congregational leaders as they provide leadership for small-group ministry in your congregation.
2. Pray for the small-group leaders whom God will raise among you. Pray for discernment in choosing the leaders. Encourage those whom you believe have the gifts and integrity to lead.
3. Pray for potential participants. Develop a list of people you wish to invite to an existing or yet-to-be-formed small group for discipleship.

Chapter Five
Processes, Practical Skills, and Persistence

Processes

Small-group life inevitably involves engaging in certain processes at different points in time. You may be called on to make decisions, solve problems, or manage conflict. You may be asked to choose whether to use available curriculum materials or to develop your own. The pastor and leaders of small groups are expected to have a plan for spiritual leadership development or for ordering the life of the group. Even the whole cycle of planning, designing, implementing, evaluating, and redesigning involves processes that will help ensure the continuing life of congregational small groups. Building your knowledge and sharpening your skills around these processes is therefore critical for effective functioning of groups.

Spiritual Discernment

As Christian disciples, we naturally seek the things of God. Spiritual discernment, therefore, is almost second nature to us. But is it? Spiritual discernment is a process in which we actively seek and try to know God's will in all matters and things. Matthew 7:7 promises: "Ask, and it will be given you; search, and you will find; knock, and the door will be opened for you." Thus, we must actively seek, pursue, and discern the will of God for us.

What shall we seek, then? In 1 Chronicles 16:11, David enjoins Israel to "seek the LORD and his strength, seek his presence continually." In his instruction to his son Solomon, David says: "Now therefore in the sight of all Israel, the assembly of the LORD, and in the hearing of our God, observe and search out all the commandments of the LORD your God; that you may possess this good land, and leave it for an inheritance to your children after you forever" (1 Chronicles 28:8).

For those who seek the Lord, God's kingdom and precepts, and things that are above with their whole heart, soul, and strength, the Lord's joy and gladness are there to enjoy. They will understand God's justice (Proverbs 28:5) and will be rewarded by the Lord (Hebrews 11:6). In Matthew 6:33, the writer urges us to "strive first for the kingdom of God and his righteousness, and all these things will be given to you as well." Discerning God's will and obeying God's precepts in everything we think, plan, say, and do will bring a harvest of peace, joy, contentment, wisdom, justice, and courage. It is also another step that brings us closer to our goal of becoming Christ-like, because Jesus himself was the epitome of that kind of life. "I can do nothing on my own. As I hear, I judge; and my judgment is just, because I seek to do not my own will but the will of him who sent me" (John 5:30).

Within your small groups, practice spiritual discernment together as you pray and search the Scriptures. Discuss your experiences with one another and reflect on them. Encourage one another, and seek God's presence while making decisions, solving problems, or handling conflicts. In a retreat setting, you may provide both the experience and hands-on training on spiritual discernment for your small-group leaders, who will later do the same with their members.

Planning and Action Cycle

On the surface, the cycle of planning, designing, implementing, evaluating, and redesigning may appear to be linear. However, this needs to be seen more as a spiral, a cycle, a never-ending process of looking for places where the presence and grace of God have not been felt or witnessed. In reality, we need to do small or daily assessments to know whether we are being open to God's leading. That is, we need to be open and flexible enough to make changes even in the way we plan, design, implement, or adapt; and we should not wait a long time to do the overall assessment. All of these processes are vital to the healthy functioning of the group. If the group ignores even one of these, there is room for rust to build up and weaken the link.

On the other hand, the group does not have to be tied down to these processes, leaving no room for God to work in and through the small group. Remember, we work in partnership with God through the Holy Spirit. However, we cannot afford to be slothful or neglectful in using God's gifts to plan and order our life together.

The spiritual disciplines of prayer, fasting, reading and studying the Scriptures, theological reflection, and caring for one another teach us how to order our lives toward a deeper and mature faith.

Planning and designing require a time set for waiting and discerning where God is directing and leading us. It is a time for reflecting on the strengths and areas of improvement for our group life. It is also a time to listen to one another in ways that build the community and help us move toward healing and wholeness.

Implementing and reviewing our goals, as a congregation and as a small group within that congregation, require leaders and members to be vigilant and to remain centered on our vision and mission. It is easy to lose the focus and go our own way if we do not share a common vision and judge what we do and how we do it against that vision.

Training in these areas, therefore, may include developing one's vision and mission, planning and designing various ministries, developing and implementing a system of accountability, and evaluating and providing feedback for improving our ministries.

Spiritual Leader Development

Spiritual discernment is especially crucial in developing leaders, whether potential or actual. How do you choose people who will be given the responsibility to lead small groups? This is not an easy matter. The kind of leaders you tap and develop will affect or influence the nature and direction of the life of the small groups they will handle. Suffice it to say that leading a small group is a ministry and calling. The task of identifying leaders needs to be wrapped in much prayer and to be directed by Divine wisdom.

Topics or issues for continued growth may include biblical guidelines for choosing leaders, scriptural qualities of leaders, and practicing spiritual disciplines.

Resource Development

Which resources to use for small-group meetings is a question often asked and for which there are no pat answers. Determining the kind of materials you will use starts with knowing what your group needs in order to grow more mature in their faith and Christian discipleship. A list of suggested resources and where to find them is on page 79.

Sometimes it is possible to tap your own members. Ask your Christian education director, pastor, or lay preacher if they know about, have used, or even have the skills and qualifications to develop resources that are adapted to your situation and needs.

Accountability and evaluation are needed at every step in the cycle.

Processes for Effective Group Life

Making decisions, solving problems, and managing conflict each require different sets of skills. In small-group life, you can hardly escape from making decisions. From the small decision of when and where to meet to the larger task of developing the group's vision and mission, members engage in decision-making. Leaders and members, therefore, need to be oriented, at the least, to the process of group decision-making, if not given training, particularly when dealing with larger issues.

Problems and conflicts are also an inevitable part of group life. Problems and conflicts have as many causes as there are ways of handling them. Both leaders and participants need to develop their skills in problem solving, conflict management, and mediation. Because this is a specialized topic, it may be helpful to invite a counselor or others trained in human dynamics to provide training in dealing with conflict.

Practical Skills

Closely related to the processes already mentioned are some practical skills that, when mastered, will contribute to the healthy and smooth functioning of the group. The processes discussed in the previous section relate either to occasional needs or to the overall plan and design for group life. In contrast, the skills discussed in this section are those that are critical almost every time you meet and interact with one another.

Leading Bible Studies

If your group includes the study of Scriptures every time you meet, and you expect to rotate leadership among members, it would certainly benefit the members if they were all given training in this area. Topics could include leader preparation, choice of curriculum materials, various methods of studying and reflecting on Scriptures in a group setting, and ways of encouraging participation and application of learning in daily life. Leading group Bible studies does not mean talking all the time. One-way communication from teacher/ leader to small-group members has never been the most effective or most appealing way to teach and learn, although it may be most convenient for the teacher. When all members actively participate or are given an opportunity to share in the reflection process, learning becomes more personal, intimate, and meaningful. With fewer people in a small group, both leading and sharing can be less overwhelming and intimidating. Because of the group's size, small-group settings are more conducive to participation than just sitting and listening passively to the leader's lecture or preaching.

Leading Prayer

How many times have you heard people say they do not know how to pray? Whenever I hear that and probe a little more, people say they mean praying in public. That includes both large and small settings. People have different notions of how prayer should sound. Some think prayer should be long, in poetic language, or worded well. For this reason alone, praying in public seems to be a formidable task that is reserved only for the stouthearted, educated, articulate, and experienced. Nothing could be further from the truth.

Proverbs 15:8-9 says that the Lord hears the prayers of the righteous and the upright. Prayer is a matter of the heart, not of the mouth. You may utter the most eloquent prayer, but your heart may not be in it. On the other hand, your prayer may be a simple, one-sentence prayer that involves your mind, body, heart, soul, and spirit.

For those who seem intimidated by the act of praying in public, you should tell them in advance that they will be leading the prayer. You may encourage them to compose their prayer at first and then to be more extemporaneous as they gain more confidence. Rotation of prayer leaders can be done alphabetically (*A* to *Z* or vice versa), oldest to youngest or vice versa, alternate male-female, by couples or by prayer partners (opening and closing), triads, or another appropriate configuration.

For group members who are not used to praying aloud or in public, you may take small steps to encourage them. The following ways have been tried in many different settings with participants of different backgrounds. Try the ones you think would be appropriate in your situation.

Silent Prayers

After the group members have told concerns around the circle, either aloud or written on a piece of paper, give them the following directions: "Pray silently for the needs of the person (a) to your right, (b) to your left, (c) across the table from you, and so forth."

Word or Phrase Prayers

Use a word (an adjective or a noun) or a phrase to extol the nature of God: Holy, Almighty, Creator, Divine, Loving, Kind, Powerful, Compassionate.

Thank Jesus for what he has done for you: one, two, or three things for which you are grateful. "Lord, I thank you for…"

Sentence Prayers

Invite participants to pray aloud a prayer of thanks or petition that is one sentence long. You may provide the following model: "O Lord, today I give you thanks for…," or, "Lord, today I pray that…"

Printed Prayers

Recite together or individually any of the following:
- A short Scripture passage, such as a Psalm
- The Lord's Prayer
- A hymn, praise song, or short chorus
- A prayer from a devotional guide
- An inspirational religious poem

Praying Through the Arts

Delight and surprise await you as you discover the depth and breadth of talents and gifts within your circle. Try the following: drawing; sketching; coloring or painting; composing a poem, hymn, or short chorus; making a collage; playing a musical instrument; dramatic reading; singing; dancing; flower arranging; making a quilt; taking nature photographs; journaling; making banners; writing a short story; or working with clay, construction paper, glue, cloth, wire, or any material to express your thoughts. This can be your prayer.

I experienced this when I was attending a retreat. Pastels were lying on the table, and I got curious because I had never used them. Using the pastels, I drew my reflection on a Scripture passage. Although I was allergic to the pastels, I discovered a wonderful way of praying through this medium. All of our talents are a gift from God, so it is only appropriate to use them to glorify, honor, praise, and thank God.

Picture Prayers

Put pictures and images on a table; then let group members choose one that best shows or expresses how they have felt God's presence and provision during an immediate past event, day, week, month, and so forth.

Nature Prayer

Pick a part of nature or creation that reminds you of the nature of God and the glory, majesty, power, grace, love, peace, wisdom, and joy of the Lord. Focus on that image while thanking God the Creator, Jesus the Redeemer, and Holy Spirit the Sustainer for who they are and what they have done in your life.

Praying the Colors

Use colors to express or remind you of things for which to pray. For example, red is for joys and celebration; blue is for people, places, and situations needing God's peace; green is for those needing God's hope or growth in discipleship; brown is for the healing and wholeness of the earth and the whole of creation; white is for life of holiness, purity, obedience, and faithfulness; yellow is for God's light shining in places of darkness (the confused mind, the depressed human spirit); purple is for heads of nations; and so on.

Communication Skills: Verbal

Verbal communication seems easy and uncomplicated. You will understand one another as long as you speak the same language, right? Wrong! Verbal communication is a complex and complicated process that involves both actual messages (the straightforward combination of letters into words and words into phrases and sentences to express thoughts) and perceived messages (interpreted). When misunderstanding and miscommunication occur, we often find that the actual and perceived messages were running in parallel but different tracks, instead of converging at some point to achieve oneness in meaning. Confusion, tension, chaos, and pain become the inevitable result of misunderstanding. Even when you exercise the best of care and sensitivity in stating your ideas, opinions, and feelings, misinterpretation may still occur.

It is important for leaders, facilitators, and participants to understand the dynamics of verbal communication and the pitfalls for misunderstanding. As our community becomes more diverse in its social, cultural, linguistic, economic, intellectual, religious, and political makeup, being able to communicate across and between these lines is an important skill to have. We cannot afford to be dogmatic and define the world according to our perspective alone. We are not the center of the world and our community. Christ is the center, and we need to understand that and live it out.

So be mindful of what you say. In the end, it is not your eloquence that will be your witness to God's love and saving grace but your life lived out of a Christian centering.

Communication Skills: Nonverbal

Adding the nonverbal layer to our verbal communication complicates the whole communication process even more. People watch our facial expressions, eye movement and focus, hand gestures, body posture and movement while they listen to what we are saying verbally. Do they match or complement one another? If so, the message we send through our lips is confirmed by our actions. The greater the complementarity between verbal and nonverbal, the clearer and stronger the message will be. The greater the contradiction, the more confusing and suspect the message becomes. When that happens, our tendency is to put more weight on the action than on the words.

So watch not only what you say but also how you say it. In a small-group setting, the complication is multiplied greatly compared with one-on-one communication. The beauty and miracle of it, though, is that even with billions of human beings on this planet, it is still not total chaos, although we cannot discount the fact that our relationships and communication are becoming more and more precarious all the time. The challenge for us is to learn to live together in Christian community and to weave into our verbal and nonverbal communication God's "love, joy, peace, patience, kindness, generosity, faithfulness, gentleness, and self-control. [For] there is no law against such things" (Galatians 5:22-23).

Listening Skills

Listening is one of the seemingly easiest skills to learn and apply in our lives, but it is the most difficult. For one thing, most of us have not had consistent, intentional, and focused training on listening. Listening requires more than just being able to hear sounds. Our ears must be able to discriminate the noise from the real message; then our brain needs to interpret that message. Depending on what is required of us in terms of response, we may agree intellectually, change our attitude, or act on what we have heard. It is not just the physical aspect of listening that is important when we are in small groups. Listening from the heart is more crucial. And people are smart enough to see through our motives.

Do we listen in order to have something to tell through the grapevine, or do we make an effort to understand where others' pain is coming from? Do we listen to find fault and build our arsenal of rebuttals, or do we seek to forgive and be reconciled with one another? Do we listen to be polite, or do we truly celebrate, without envy, when others tell about their joys? Do we listen with our hearts?

Human Relations Skills

When group members come from different backgrounds, cross-cultural communication may occur. As they exchange messages and interact with one another in the group, their background, experiences, language, customs, traditions, and other kinds of affiliations will come to bear. Therefore, it is crucial that they learn to respect one another. When group members disagree with one another, it is more productive if they control the urge to contradict everything the others say. Practicing hospitality and being open-minded can contribute more to healing and reconciliation, as well as to more-satisfying interpersonal relationships, than being disagreeable and combative. Remember, you do not have the monopoly to the right answer. Always have room for other perspectives, however bitter the pill may be to your taste.

Group Facilitation Skills

If you are the leader, it will be to your advantage to learn how to facilitate group processes. Learning takes time and needs to be continuous throughout your life. Each group has a different personality;

therefore, you will need to adjust and adapt how you facilitate group processes every time the composition or size of the group changes. Being sensitive to the needs of the group as a whole and of individual members will help you determine how to proceed.

Usually, small groups are more informal, so one-way communication from leader to group is usually not the best approach. If you insist on lecturing or preaching, group members may not listen to or follow you. You may even lose credibility among the participants. Or, worse, some may stop coming.

Resist the tendency to dominate the conversation. Provide equal opportunity for all members to tell their faith stories, reflection on the subject matter, or joys and concerns. If some members love to hear themselves talk, gently remind them to give others a chance to speak. You may need to encourage the reticent to join in the conversation. In any case, the leader needs to constantly monitor participation of all members and to intervene if necessary.

Having an agenda will help the group process flow smoothly, although you do not have to be restrained by it. Keep within the time allotted for each item on the agenda. This intent needs to be communicated at the start of the meeting. Moreover, in order to avoid confusion and misunderstanding, discuss your expectations of one another, either for a particular meeting or for the entire life of your group.

Having an agenda will help the group process flow smoothly.

Critical Thinking Skills

Whenever members of the small group reflect on a Scripture passage or a recent event and discuss its significance and relevance to their daily living as Christian disciples, they are engaging in critical thinking. Whenever they try to discern God's will or call and weigh consequences of certain actions and decisions, they are doing critical thinking. Whenever they tackle questions such as why, how, so what, for what purpose, or if...then what, they are thinking critically. Therefore, it is important that leaders and members continue to sharpen these skills to help them explore all possibilities, alternatives, and perspectives. Thus, they will be able to use their God-given ability to think and reason and will be less tempted to settle for one limited explanation, interpretation, or solution.

Administrative Skills

Administrative skills are called for when planning, organizing, and coordinating activities and work of members, as well as when implementing the plans. Follow-up is also a necessary part of the leader's job. Most of all, linking every activity to the overall vision, mission, goals, and focus of the group is essential as group members grow and mature together.

The pastor and coordinator of the church's small-group ministry are usually the people who need to hone their administrative skills the most. To some degree, every small-group leader needs administrative skills.

Creativity

All work and no play leads to stress and burnout. Use all your creative powers when planning small-group activities, in order to keep them interesting. Try to use different kinds of music and musical instruments, poetry, visual arts, and other artistic forms as part of your worship and praise to God. Use various symbols (be sure to explain their meanings) and objects that will appeal to the different senses during worship, prayer, Bible study, singing, fellowship.

Being creative keeps you from getting stale and falling into a rut. It keeps the level of interest high so that members will return again and again. It encourages exploration and use of God-given talents and energizes, enlivens, and stimulates sharing.

Persistence

Great strides in science and technology, as well as pressure to get ahead and be number one, have created both an expectation and a demand for instant gratification. We have grown accustomed to having what we want now. Youth sometimes get tired of the repeated reminders of the more senior generation that the pace of life has speeded up so much. The older ones advise the younger ones to be patient and to wait. Some things just take time, and you cannot force them to keep abreast with your own pace. In Ecclesiastes 3:1, we are reminded that "for everything there is a season, and a time for every matter under heaven."

Growing and building your small-group ministry is like farming. The farmer uses mechanized and non-mechanized implements to prepare the ground by loosening the earth, turning it upside down, and making it breathe. The soil is cleared of unwanted debris and rocks and then is tilled and prepared. Experience has given the farmer wisdom not to sow seeds before this step is completed. After the earth has been prepared, seeds that have gone through a process of preparation are sowed. During the germination stage underground, the surface of the soil does not indicate that anything is happening to the seed or the soil. Finally, visible signs of growth that have begun underneath the earth can be seen. The tiny shoots push up through a crack in the ground and reach for the sunlight and the air while the roots push down to search for water and other nutrients in the soil. The plant grows taller and deeper, until one day it starts to bear flowers, then fruits. All the while, the farmer watches the crop, tends it, waters it, and feeds it with the right amount of food at the right time so that it will grow and yield a great harvest. All of these things do not happen overnight. It takes a season to complete the cycle of tilling, sowing, tending, growing, bearing, maturing, and harvesting.

So it is with congregational small groups, especially if your faith community has not had the vision for Christian discipleship, nurture, and care through that ministry. While we may hear about churches that have grown or are growing into the thousands through the use of small groups, it is likely that they have gone through a period of preparation and waiting, as well as of praying and working while waiting. Perseverance is definitely another key to growing your small-group ministry. It is easy to get discouraged and disheartened when no one seems to be catching the vision or growing in number and participation. It is difficult to continue when the grand vision seems to have fizzled out.

Remember, there is a time for germination. Do not give up on communicating the vision—through the pulpit, one-on-one conversations, consultations with experts and with church staff, small groups and key lay leaders, surveys, teaching moments, reading, and your own enthusiasm and modeling of small-group life. Before you ask others to try building Christian community, nurturing their faith, sharing and caring through small groups, be sure you, the leader or pastor, have had or are having that experience yourself. Your own experience of how a small group has helped you grow in your faith and in your love for others is the most powerful testimony you can ever tell. Some leaders start small, with one or two small groups of key congregational leaders who share the vision and continue, persistently and consistently, to practice the spiritual disciplines and set an example of caring and sharing within and outside their group until others catch the vision. This small band of leaders also continues their education about growing in faith, group dynamics, leadership, making decisions, solving problems, engaging in ministries of justice and compassion, and other relevant topics. All these are part of the preparation, perseverance, and working while waiting. Thus, when the vision finally catches on, the leadership will be in place and can face up to the challenge. Great small-group participation, with spiritually mature leaders, is a recipe for growth and transformation.

In short, be not disheartened. Persist. Let not your heart faint. Persevere. Be of good courage, for the Lord your God is with you. Be patient and long-suffering. If you have committed yourself to

Perseverance is an important key to growing your small-group ministry.

being available as God's partner in ministry and growing spiritually through the power of the Holy Spirit, count on Christ's being "with you always, to the end of the age" (Matthew 28:20). If you are disappointed, ask yourself why and what it is that you are disappointed about. Is it because you want results? If so, why and what kind of results? If you are afraid, ask yourself why you are afraid and what it is that you are afraid of. Are you afraid of failure? If so, why? Do you see failure as a reflection on your abilities and skills as a leader? If so, why?

God wants us to learn to completely depend on God (Proverbs 3:5). Follow God's lead faithfully, and let the Lord of the harvest take care of the yield.

Chapter Six
Assessment

very time I travel, it helps to have clear and specific directions from where I am to my destination. In order to get anywhere, it helps to know where you are in relation to your destination, whether you are in a multilevel mall, in a hospital, in a hotel, in the air, in the ocean, or in a new territory. Knowing that, as well as your goal and purpose for your trip, will aid you in mapping out the best route. When changing planes, the first thing I do is locate where I am at the airport terminal. I look on the map for the dot or arrow with the corresponding message "You are here"; then I locate my next departure gate. Depending on the time and options available, I decide how to get to my next gate in the most time- and energy-efficient manner.

That is also the way it is with small-group ministry. It would help to know where you are—in terms of vision, mission, attitude, spiritual readiness, knowledge, and training—before you move in the direction God is leading you. In this chapter and in the next, we will be looking at an assessment tool to help you determine where you are in relation to the church's primary task. In this chapter, I will explain the vertical and horizontal dimensions of our faith journey, as well as the nature, strengths, and weaknesses of each possible scenario. In the next chapter, we will look more closely at the different ways we can move, as a group, from where we are to where God wants us to be.

Union

Relationship With God Through Christ

Restoration

Separation

The Vertical Dimension: Relationship With God Through Christ

The vertical axis represents our growing relationship with God through Jesus Christ. As in a journey, we move from a state of separation to restoration and, finally, into full union with God.

Separation includes anything and everything that distances us from God. It involves not just the spiritual aspect but rather our entire being. In the spiritual domain, our sins separate us from the love of God: "There is no distinction, since all have sinned and fall short of the glory of God" (Romans 3:22-23). Isaiah 59:2 says: "Your iniquities have been barriers between you and your God, and your sins have hidden his face from you so that he does not hear." When we allow our sins and feelings of guilt to keep us away from God, we stand to lose.

Joining others in corporate worship helps us draw closer to God, so we need to make sure that the time we reserve for worship is not choked up by the busyness of life and other cares. Otherwise, we may be physically and spiritually alienating ourselves from the Divine presence. This is not to say that God's presence is not with us outside of worship time. Indeed, we can worship God anytime and anyplace. However, a certain dynamic is present when we worship amongst God's people.

We can be separated from God in many ways. What keeps you from getting to know God? What are your excuses for not spending time in prayer, worship, study of God's Word, participation in the Lord's Supper? What are your reasons for not growing in your love for God? What would help restore your relationship with God?

Restoration moves us closer to God. Jesus Christ's self-giving love, through his death on the cross, restores us into full relationship with God: "It will be reckoned to us who believe in him who raised Jesus our Lord from the dead, who was handed over to death for our trespasses and was raised for our justification. Therefore, since we are justified by faith, we have peace with God through our Lord Jesus Christ, through whom we have obtained access to this grace in which we stand" (Romans 4:24–5:2). The cross serves as the bridge of love between us and God, who is holy. When we acknowledge and repent of our sin, as well as ask and receive forgiveness, healing takes place (Psalm 32:5). Wholeness in our relationship with God means that restoration and healing have taken place in all dimensions of our life.

Union with Christ is having the mind of Christ and being Christlike, as well as being one with God in Christ (John 17:20-26). Our continuing journey in discipleship, with the aid of God's sanctifying grace, helps us move toward perfection and toward unity in the Spirit.

Growing Deep and Strong

The means of grace help us grow deeper and move in progression along the different points on the axis, from separation to restoration to union with God through Christ. They are also expressions or manifestations of such growth. In other words, when we participate in the means of grace, we experience transformation and a deepening in our faith. On the other hand, that same transformation and growth in discipleship will create an ever-increasing hunger to participate in the means of grace and to practice the spiritual disciplines. They function, therefore, as both enhancers and as evidence of our maturing Christian faith.

I invite your group to go through this list and, for every spiritual discipline, ask these questions:

1. How often have we participated in or practiced this?
2. Whenever we have participated in or practiced this, how has it helped us experience transformation and growth in our faith in God through Jesus Christ?
3. How has it helped us in our daily walk as Christian disciples?
4. If we have never done/practiced this before, what is keeping us from doing it?
5. How can we be more intentional in incorporating this spiritual discipline into our small-group life?
6. What obstacles need to be removed?

Traditional means of grace include
- **doing good,**
- **avoiding evil,**
- **worship,**
- **Bible study,**
- **fasting,**
- **Christian conferencing,**
- **Holy Communion,**
- **prayer.**

The Horizontal Dimension:
Relationship With Our Neighbors

The horizontal axis represents our relationship with others. As with the vertical axis, our relationship with our neighbor also moves from separation to restoration to union with one another in Christ. Neighbor includes everyone other than yourself. They may be members of your own immediate family, your next-door neighbors, friends, extended family, members of your own faith community, as well as those belonging outside your social, economic, religious, educational, cultural, political, or special-interest circles. Even our enemies are our neighbors.

Separation from others may be brought about by physical, emotional, intellectual, material, or cultural differences and conflicts. Misunderstanding, fear, pride, suspicion, hatred, indifferent attitude, or unforgiving spirit can keep us from having a peaceful and harmonious relationship with others. As with our relationship with God, becoming whole in our relationship with our neighbor involves restoration and healing in all dimensions of our connection points with others.

Relationship With Our Neighbors

Separation, Restoration, Union

Restoration helps us move toward reconciliation with our neighbor. Offering and receiving forgiveness become crucial steps in the process of healing and wholeness. When we begin to see one another as Christ sees us—precious in his sight—we can respect, honor, accept, listen to, and love one another as Christ loves us.

Union is being one with one another in and through Christ, sharing in agape love, and living in peace with one another:

> If then there is any encouragement in Christ, any consolation from love, any sharing in the Spirit, any compassion and sympathy, make my joy complete: be of the same mind, having the same love, being in full accord and of one mind. Do nothing from selfish ambition or conceit, but in humility regard others as better than yourselves. Let each of you look not to your own interests, but to the interests of others. Let the same mind be in you that was in Christ Jesus. (Philippians 2:1-5)

It is more possible to live in peace and harmony with people with whom we are familiar, those within our comfort zone, than with those with whom we are not familiar. We tend to exclude those we fear, look down on, disagree with, do not know, do not understand. We may even resist the idea of sharing God's saving grace with them. However, the call to love not only God but also our neighbor as we love ourselves has remained unchanged. In a culture where individualism and personal achievement are glorified, loving others as Christ loves us presents a bigger challenge. A tension exists between attitudes such as "I can do it myself" and "I don't need you," on the one hand, and "I need you" and "We can do this together," on the other.

Growing Deep and Strong

As with the vertical axis, participating in the means of grace will help restore, deepen, and strengthen your relationship with others, as well as expand your circle, particularly in your movement toward the goal of allowing the unity of the Spirit to prevail in your relationships and life together. That same growth will find expression in an increased desire to participate in and practice the spiritual disciplines more and more each day.

Use the following questions to help your group evaluate its participation in the means of grace from a relational perspective:

1. Is this means of grace an integral part of our efforts to build Christian community? If so, how has this helped us grow deep and strong in our relationship with each member of our group?

2. How has this means of grace helped us establish, restore, deepen, or strengthen our relationship with those outside our group?

3. How can we use this means of grace to expand the boundaries of our circle and/or to help form new circles?

4. How can this means of grace help us in sharing our faith with others?

5. If we have not practiced this means of grace before, what is keeping us from doing it?

6. How can we be more intentional in making this means of grace an integral part of our group life?

Assessing the Christian Spiritual Formation Needs of Small Groups

Understanding the vertical and horizontal dimensions of small-group life is only the first step in using this assessment tool. The next step is to integrate these two axes to form four possible combinations or quadrants. Two elements are critical: intentionality and the role of the Holy Spirit.

Is your group coming together with the intention and desire to get to know God, learn/discern God's will, and live out God's will in the way you care for, build up, and love one another? In other words, is your group intentionally making the connection between love of God and love of others? Is there balance between the two axes? This is the foundation for our growth in Christian discipleship. Even when your group has been formed to carry out a particular task, love of God and of neighbor needs to be the underlying standard against which your work is to be measured.

A second and more important element is the work of the Holy Spirit. Even when you completely understand your call as a group or faith community to love God and neighbor, and even when you intentionally make sure that the relationship between the two is always before you, there will be an emptiness and a vacuum if the Holy Spirit cannot work freely in and through your life, individually and corporately. It will feel like a constant striving without direction. Allowing space for the Holy Spirit to have the freedom to move and shape you according to God's design is, therefore, crucial.

Quadrant One: Growing in Love of God; Not Growing in Love of Others

Nature

Groups that fall in Quadrant One spend their time engaging in practices and spiritual disciplines that enable them to walk closely with God. Perhaps their whole life is lived in an attitude of prayer, worship, and humility before the Lord; of constantly discerning God's will; of lifting up God's name. That is commendable. Examples of groups that tend to be in Quadrant One are Bible study groups, Sunday school classes, study groups on the lectionary or other theological resources, prayer and meditation groups, praise and worship groups, retreat or spiritual formation groups.

Although these groups have a clear and distinct upward reach, they do not intentionally make the connection and keep a balance between spiritual growth and all other dimensions of life. Group members often neglect or are not concerned about building Christian community that includes all people. They may be growing spiritually, but the fruits of the Spirit are sorely lacking.

Possible Dangers

In this scenario, the group immerses itself in learning about and knowing God intimately. Intellectual knowledge about God, as well as the experience of the holy, may be increasing daily. However, that intimacy with God does not find full expression in their relationships with family, friends, coworkers, strangers, and the disenfranchised. Their language may be peppered with Christian language, thus exuding an aura of holiness, but some may be authentic and some may not. Only God can judge the heart.

Another danger groups need to be aware of is developing spiritual smugness. Just because the group studies the Bible and prays together, while others do not appear to make the same commitment, does not make group members any better than others. Members may develop a judgmental attitude toward those who do not seem to be focusing on spiritual things. They may place a higher value or worth on what their group does or focuses on. When that attitude prevails, they set themselves apart as if they have more worth or more favor with God. A good antidote to this pharisaic syndrome is to remind ourselves constantly of Jesus' parable about the Pharisee and the tax collector who went up to the temple to pray: "The Pharisee, standing by himself, was praying thus, 'God, I thank you that I am not like other people: thieves, rogues, adulterers, or even like this tax collector. I fast twice a week; I give a tenth of all my income'" (Luke 18:11-12). And Jesus' stinging reminder is this: "I tell you, this [tax collector] went down to his home justified rather than the [Pharisee]; for all who exalt themselves will be humbled, but all who humble themselves will be exalted" (Luke 18:14). Indeed, pride is a sin that brings us right back to the start: separation from God.

Another danger is that members may develop an elitist or exclusionist attitude. "Your values are different from ours," they might say. In that case, openness and acceptance may not be evident, and people who do not belong to the group may feel alienated, not welcome, and not heard. Outsiders may then view the group as too holy and pure for them and not even worth a try.

Lastly, separation of Christian spirituality from ministry in daily life may lead to accepting and engaging in certain acts that are contrary to biblical mandates. In the worst cases, Scripture may even be used to rationalize hate and exclude certain groups.

Quadrant Two: Not Growing in Love of God; Not Growing in Love of Others

Nature

Quadrant Two groups, either by design or intention, pay little attention to and have little interest in a deepening relationship with both God and others. And they have no intention of bringing the two dimensions together. By design, I mean groups that are given specific responsibilities and tasks to complete, some that are short-term and others that are long-term. They work together for purposes other than practicing the spiritual disciplines or having fellowship with one another. Groups that tend to find themselves in Quadrant Two are church committees and councils, task forces, trustees, choirs, guilds, staff groups, planning groups, and administrative groups. It is possible in these settings to have prayers, whether perfunctory or sincere, before and/or after the meeting. Fellowship is also inevitable, but that is not the main goal or motivation for being together. By intention, I mean groups with members who come just because their name is on the list and they have been assigned a task. But strengthening relationships among members or with God is not on their agenda. Basically, the group is just a collection of individuals who do not see themselves as having a future together as far as Christian community is concerned.

Quadrant Two:
Not Growing in
Love of God;
Not Growing in
Love of Others

Possible Dangers

If the group has been convened for a specific purpose, their task may be seen as more important than a continuing growth in the faith and in relationships with one another, especially if they can achieve the latter in other settings. Moreover, their task may not be viewed as a form of ministry where partnership with God and neighbor is critical. A similar danger is to separate the task from spirituality and Christian community and caring.

In an individualistic culture, it is tempting to develop an attitude of indifference to God and neighbor: "We don't care as long as we complete our job. That's what we're called to do." Members may develop an attitude of arrogance and self-sufficiency: "Thanks, but we can make it on our own. We don't need your help." It may not be as blatant as that, but that is what the attitude implies. In the worst cases, there may even be fights, gossip, intrigues, festering and unresolved conflicts, whining, territoriality, division, factionalism, and degeneration of relationships.

Quadrant Three: Not Growing in Love of God; Growing in Love of Others

Nature

Groups in Quadrant Three have as their main purpose the strengthening of relationships among people within and/or outside the group, but there is no accompanying concern with their faith formation and Christian discipleship. Members are in tune with the needs of one another, the group, and the larger community. Building community, not necessarily Christian community, is a high priority. Groups that are in Quadrant Three are likely to engage primarily in parties, group recreational activities, entertainment, social gatherings, dining, group trips. Some support groups are in this quadrant. On occasion, the group may deliberately separate spiritual growth from fellowship and entertainment. Such groups may not want to be seen as being too religious in nature, whatever that may mean to them.

In other cases, groups that focus primarily on social justice action and deliberately strip those acts of any spiritual dimension could easily fall into this quadrant. Other groups that may find themselves in this quadrant are those with members who are constantly reaching out to others, attending to the needs of others, and going out on missions. Although they may see their work as a form of ministry, they place little emphasis on making the connection between their spiritual growth and their outreach efforts. Their outreach ministries are not done as an outgrowth of their call to Christian discipleship, the practice of spiritual disciplines, and their conviction to live out their faith in daily life.

Possible Dangers

When group members develop a belief that feeling good about their relationships or helping others is all that matters, it may be time to assess the group life and its priorities. We have grown accustomed to making a dichotomy between the human and the divine, believing that somehow human relationships are totally separate from the divine. In the same manner, we may be creating a false dichotomy between faith and works, believing that keeping them in constant tension is not necessary for Christian spiritual transformation.

It is also not healthy to put more weight on one over the other (for example, regarding outreach efforts and mission activities as more important than spiritual growth). When this happens, members may develop a judgmental attitude toward those who may appear to devote their time solely to the practice of spiritual disciplines. While the focus may be different from Quadrant One, the same smugness will be evident. Being busy with works of justice, mercy, compassion, caring, support, encouragement, relationship building, evangelism, mission, and outreach may turn into a form of idolatry. It is also likely that group members will become busybodies and suffer from burnout and feelings of resentment.

In some cases, the group focuses only on the needs of their own members and remains oblivious to the needs of the larger community. This leads to the group becoming relationally ingrown. They will not reach out and multiply, either by intention or by design.

Quadrant Four: Growing in Love of God; Growing in Love of Others

Nature

Quadrant Four groups not only balance their focus on God and their neighbors but also keep the tension and relationship between the two dimensions always active. Their journey into deepening faith evokes a response to do God's will in their daily life. As they study the Scriptures and hear the call "to do justice, and to love kindness, and to walk humbly with…God" (Micah 6:8), they accept the challenge and translate it into action steps that can be lived out. As they carry out their tasks, members accept and believe that their Christian faith needs to be expressed in the way they live, work, relate with, and care for one another. Their love for God gets expressed in their love for neighbor. Conversely, their love for neighbor is regarded as one of the ways they love God. They bear the fruits of the Spirit (Romans 12–15; 1 Corinthians 12–14; Galatians 5:22-25; Ephesians 4). They use their God-given talents, skills, and gifts to serve God and others. Their ultimate goal is unity with God and others as expressed in John 17:21: "That they may all be one. As you, Father, are in me and I am in you, may they also be in us." Unity is experienced in one body, Spirit, hope, Lord, faith, baptism, and faith in God (Ephesians 4:4-6). This unity, harmony, and growing toward spiritual maturity becomes a powerful witness for Christ and his bride, the church.

The challenge before us is how to move from separation to being restored to finally uniting fully with God and others. The goal of small-group ministries is to create and nurture groups so that they can move into and function out of Quadrant Four. The next chapter will deal with strategies for moving groups toward Quadrant Four.

Quadrant Four: Growing in Love of God; Growing in Love of Others

Assignment

Examine the small groups in your congregation and decide which quadrant each group is in.

Think about these questions:
1. What does our current situation indicate about the health of existing small-group ministries?
2. Which groups need help in moving toward Quadrant Four?
3. Which groups are in Quadrant Four?

Chapter Seven
Healthy Growth

In this chapter, we will explore some strategies to help small groups move into Quadrant Four, where the Great Commandment is intentionally lived out. Small groups that are already in Quadrant Four may need to explore ways to ensure that the group remains in this quadrant and does not begin to slide toward other quadrants.

Whether groups are formed or are forming, it is helpful to have Christ's challenge before them and to measure the purpose, nature, and growth of small groups according to the Great Commandment, the Great Commission, and the church's primary task. The challenge of keeping these two dimensions (love of God and love of neighbor) constantly in balance and tension is what will push the groups to grow into maturity.

The following section will offer your group some questions to reflect on and respond to, in order to move from your current reality to your envisioned reality. That desired reality is your vision for members of your small group to grow into full maturity and in the likeness of Christ. Your answers to the questions will provide your group the specific strategies unique to your own group, setting, and situation. No easy answers exist; however, it is in your struggle with these questions that you will find that the grace of God is sufficient for all your needs. It is up to your small group to keep yourselves open to the leading of the Holy Spirit as you discern what God is calling you to do in response to Christ's teaching to love God and love neighbor as yourself and to make disciples of all nations.

Quadrant One: Growing in Love of God; Not Growing in Love of Others

Our desire to draw closer to God honors the Spirit that is within us. We were created in the image of God; thus, we are only responding to the call of the Divine in our lives when we read, study, and meditate on the Scriptures together. We focus on the holy when we pray, praise, thank, and worship God as individuals and as a body. We grow in our understanding of God when we participate in Christian conferencing. We continue to grow amazed and in awe of the mystery of Christ's saving grace when we take Communion with fellow believers around the table. Sometimes other activities, such as praying while painting, composing, or journaling, also draw us closer to the bosom of God.

Your group members can deepen their love and worship of the Holy One in innumerable ways. Continue to explore those ways, and encourage one another in your group to grow closer to God daily. It is good if you are attending to the God-dimension in your small groups. Like the trees that are well grounded through their deep root system, your group can find strength to face the dark valleys and storms in life by growing deeper in faith. Through the strength that God provides when you are firmly rooted in the Source of your salvation, you will be able to meet the harshest, fiercest, and meanest challenges that come your way. Tests, trials, challenges, pain, and hurt are a given. They will surely come. The important thing is to keep being formed, transformed, and renewed by the power of the Holy Spirit every moment. The same strength that helps you face the storms of life will also sustain you with peace, joy, and contentment that the world has never known, experienced, or can offer.

However, if the God-dimension is the sole focus of your life as individuals and as a group, you are missing something. You are responding to only half of the Great Commandment. You have no balance. The fulcrum rests heavily on one side, causing your life to be tilted toward one direction. If your group life resides in Quadrant One, how can you help your group move toward Quadrant Four and achieve balance so that love of God finds its expression in love of neighbor? If all you do when you meet is study the Bible and worship or take Communion together, what will push you to grow in loving your neighbor?

Moving From Quadrant One to Quadrant Four

Groups in Quadrant One can use these questions to guide their movement toward Quadrant Four:

1. What is God challenging us to do in response to the Scriptures we are studying? (For example, if you are studying a passage that deals with justice issues, how are you going to apply that in your particular setting?)

Quadrant One: Growing in Love of God; Not Growing in Love of Others

Quadrant Four: Growing in Love of God; Growing in Love of Others

2. How will we live out the challenge, as individuals and as a group, this coming week?

3. What are the needs of our community? (Choose one specific need that can be your group's mission project. What specific action are you going to take to meet the identified need?)

4. Today or this week, how have we shown our love of God at home? at work? at school? at play? in the marketplace? on the road? in the hospital? in places of need such as disaster areas? in unfair and unjust situations?

5. Where have we seen God at work in our relationships with others?

6. How do we intentionally make a connection between our spiritual growth and our relationship with others?

7. What particular human relationships are we being called to restore and heal through forgiveness and sharing of our faith? What is God leading us to do? How do we respond?

8. Which individual or group do we need to touch with Jesus' love today? Who do we need to include around the Lord's table? Who needs to hear the good news of God's love through Jesus Christ?

9. Which individual or group are we excluding? Why? What stereotypes and prejudices do we hold that keep us from including and welcoming them in our community?

10. Beyond intercessory prayer, what have we done for the poor and disenfranchised today, in response to Christ's call?

11. Who are the sick, hungry, naked, and prisoners in our community? How are we ministering to them? If we are not doing anything, why are we not meeting their needs? How can we grow deep in our love for our neighbors?

12. How can we help nurture others in their faith?

13. How can we hold one another accountable as we grow in our love of God and neighbor?

14. How do we build up one another through our words and actions?

15. How do we practice what we know and believe in?

These are some of the questions that will help you extend your love of God and let it spill into your relationships with others, within and outside your own small group. It calls you to apply scriptural truths in daily living, putting muscles and flesh in your declaration of love for God. It calls you to put into practical, concrete, observable language the knowledge, beliefs, values, and attitudes you have gained about Christian living through the practice of spiritual disciplines.

It calls you to move from head and heart to hand and heel.

Quadrant Two: Not Growing in Love of God; Not Growing in Love of Others

Task groups in the church often operate mostly out of Quadrant Two. It is not that they do not need God or others or that they are not growing in their love of God and neighbor individually. While committee or ministry team members may see their work as a form of Christian service, that value and belief is not held constantly before them as they carry out their responsibilities.

Any number of committees or groups in your church may easily find themselves in this quadrant if they focus mainly on completing a certain task. For example, the choir is responsible for helping lead the worship through their musical offerings. Their work can easily be related to growth in the God-dimension. However, the group may be a candidate for Quadrant Two if all they do is practice the music for Sunday and if getting the compliments of worshipers becomes the driving force behind a flawless musical rendition, instead of a complete and exclusive worship offering to God.

The same can be true for other groups, such as the administrative council, staff/pastor-parish committee, board of trustees, committee on lay leadership, strategic planning committee, pastoral and/or administrative staff group, finance/stewardship committee, worship planning team, education committee, and so forth. Whatever the designated task of the group, it is important for the group to explore ways by which members can live in obedience to the teachings of Jesus Christ while carrying out the duties and responsibilities for the ongoing ministries of the church. Groups that find themselves in Quadrant Two are challenged to transform into groups where faith sharing, Christian discipleship and nurture, accountability, outreach and justice ministry, worship, stewardship, Christian community, teaching and learning, equipping leaders, fellowship, and support take place and are encouraged.

What would happen if every time group members met, they approached their meeting as worship and the discussion of business as part of the worship service? What would happen if the decisions, plans, and action steps were seen as outreach ministry?

Moving From Quadrant Two to Quadrant Four

Groups in Quadrant Two can use these questions to guide their movement toward Quadrant Four:

1. How do we nurture our faith whenever we meet as a group?
2. How does our group help nurture others in their faith?
3. What are the ways by which we share our faith within our group?

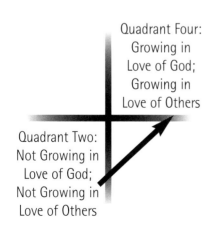

Quadrant Four: Growing in Love of God; Growing in Love of Others

Quadrant Two: Not Growing in Love of God; Not Growing in Love of Others

4. Are we practicing the spiritual disciplines and participating in the means of grace as a group? If not, why not? How will we make the means of grace an intentional part of our group life?
5. How does our group model a Christ-like life?
6. How do we, as a group, form Christian disciples?
7. How does our small group send out disciples who will make a difference in our community?
8. How are we building up one another within our group?
9. How do we extend hospitality and friendship to others?
10. How is our group reaching out to one another and to others with the love of Jesus Christ?

In one church, the choir met once a week for rehearsals. Each year, they prepared a mini-concert on special occasions. At one point, they decided to take the mini-concert to the nursing home in a neighboring town. Their experience transformed them. By stepping out of their box, they blessed a lot more lives and were blessed in return. After the concert, choir members began visiting with residents and sharing Christ's love in a variety of ways: listening, telling stories, looking at photo albums with them, holding their hands, pushing their wheelchairs, smiling, and laughing.

Once, the Girl Scout troop led by one of the members came with the choir and gave handmade crafts to the residents. In what others would consider a simple gesture, this choir not only accomplished the task they were supposed to do but also used their talents in ministering to others outside their church. In the case of the young children, the choir also set an example of loving and serving and provided role models. After the concert at the nursing home, they started going out to eat ice cream or gathering at one of the members' homes for fellowship. Before going into the sanctuary on Sunday mornings, they began offering intercessory prayers. This may be a simple example, but it shows that you can find ways, even in simple activities, to grow in your love for God and neighbor. Continue to seek and build into your group life and ministry opportunities for faith formation and outreach.

Quadrant Three: Not Growing in Love of God; Growing in Love of Others

I have seen, known, and been a part of congregational groups whose aim is to have fellowship and nothing more. It is good if we are able to build up and encourage one another through fellowship and support. Many people in this world long to be connected and to be part of something. The cultural values of independence, self-sufficiency, charting your own course, personal determination, and success run counter to our human nature to be connected with and supported by one another. We may have gone too far on the individualistic end of the relationship spectrum. When we provide settings where individuals feel welcomed, accepted, safe, and valued, those famished for relationships will often grab the opportunity and soak up everything like a dry sponge. Small groups offering fellowship, support, entertainment, and friendship become attractive to them. Some will join expecting the group to offer them food, fun, frolic, and fellowship, but nothing more.

One danger with children, youth, singles, young adults, married couples, senior adults, or any other group that focuses on providing only fun activities for the members is that faith matters are not given equal attention. If that is all the group does, members might as well join any civic or social club. As a faith community, we are called to balance discipleship with fellowship, spirituality with building community, faith with fruits.

Moving from Quadrant Three to Quadrant Four

Groups can use these questions to explore providing balance between fellowship and faith formation:

1. What are the spiritual needs of our group members, and how can we meet those needs?
2. What creative ways can be used to introduce the vertical dimension?
3. What are the sources of resistance? Why have members shied away from developing a relationship with God?
4. How can we introduce, with compassion, the need for tending the God-dimension in our life as a group?
5. How can we encourage others to see that fullness of life can be experienced when both love of God and love of neighbor are fully expressed in our life together?

Quadrant Four: Growing in Love of God; Growing in Love of Others

Quadrants One, Two, and Three lack balance in one way or another. Therefore, groups that find themselves in any of these quadrants are encouraged to examine their current reality and seek ways to move to Quadrant Four, where there is balance between the vertical and horizontal dimensions. However, when you believe that your group has crossed the threshold into Quadrant Four, it does not mean that you have arrived. Anytime you become stagnant and stale, you may slip back into another quadrant or start to feel smug. Your group

Quadrant Four:
Growing in
Love of God;
Growing in
Love of Others

Quadrant Three:
Not Growing in
Love of God;
Growing in Love
of Others

should not stop and become complacent and self-satisfied. You need to be constantly seeking God's direction and allowing the Holy Spirit to inspire and fire you up so that you may continue to grow into full maturity and unity.

Staying in Quadrant Four

Quadrant Four: Growing in Love of God; Growing in Love of Others

Groups in Quadrant Four can use these questions to help keep focused on loving God and loving neighbor:

1. What other avenues have we not yet explored in expressing our love of God and of neighbor? (Think outside your box.)
2. How can we maintain our Christ-centeredness while strengthening our relationships with one another?
3. Where have we become stagnant and stale? Why? What is keeping us from growing in our faith?
4. What spiritual gifts among us need to be tapped, developed, and used for building up one another and extending God's kingdom within and outside our community?
5. Today, as a group, how did we express and grow in our love for God and neighbor? How have lives been touched? How has our love for God and others made a difference?

As you struggle with these questions, remember that change and growth do not happen overnight. It is a process that takes time. You will have to take each person where he or she is and then take the time to develop healthy relationships with one another and with God through Jesus Christ.

The questions listed in this chapter are just a starting point. Members of the small groups will need to prayerfully assess where they are and prayerfully discern God's will as to how they are going to obey Christ's mandate to love God and love neighbor as they love themselves.

Chapter Eight
Putting It All Together

he process of building and growing your small-group ministry has four steps: assessing, accessing, progressing, and recasting. In this chapter, we will define the steps and discuss how they interact with one another.

Assessing

Assessing is defining your current reality and developing a vision for your small-group ministry. The quadrants described in Chapters Six and Seven are a tool that you can use to evaluate your situation. The assessment step is crucial, for it is nearly impossible to move forward if you do not know where you are.

In the assessment step, a planning group such as the administrative council or a small-group ministry task force begins to develop and formulate a vision for your congregation. Studying the nature and needs of your faith community does not happen overnight. You need to ask a lot of questions—of yourselves, of the rest of the leaders, and of your congregation. Casting and communicating the vision may include sermons challenging the congregation to think a new way, not business as usual. It may also include surveys and conversations with groups within your church. Help members reflect on what they believe God is challenging them to do and how that may be lived out. Ask why you, as a church, exist. What does it mean to be a church, according to Scripture? What do you, as a body, want to be as a community of faith? How can you best embody that vision?

Scripture study and prayer are part of the discernment process in developing a vision. Explore your call as the body of Christ in your particular setting. What would it take to transform your congregation from one with a collection of small groups to one where all have a common vision of loving God and loving neighbor, within the context of the mission of making disciples?

Challenge individuals and the congregation to envision each group they belong to as a place for spiritual formation, equipping for discipleship, sharing faith, teaching and learning, building Christian community, and engaging in ministry in daily life. Start with families and with each existing group in your church. Communicate the vision whenever, wherever, and with whomever you can. While you are doing this, your planning group needs to model for the rest of the congregation that vision. Again, you may start with your own family and with your planning group. You cannot ask any member or group to do what you are not willing to do yourself. Besides, it will give authenticity to your testimony and witness when you say, "I have experienced it myself and the transformation it has brought to my life."

Review Chapters Three and Four, and examine how your planning and visioning group can incorporate the critical ingredients of small-group ministry in the life of your own group. Do you invoke the presence of the Holy Spirit in your group? Are you constantly engaged in prayer and spiritual discernment? What is your vision for your faith community, and what processes are you using to develop that vision? What are your sources of power, your roles, and your qualities as pastor and leader of small groups?

What groups already exist in your congregation? Do you have an administrative council, pastoral staff, or planning/visioning group; Sunday school classes and staff groups; choir and worship planning team; staff-parish, trustees, finance, and other committees? Do you have age-level and life-span ministries for children, youth, young adults, senior adults, singles, married couples, and families? What about women's and men's ministries; ministry groups for the poor, the homeless, children, and people with special needs; fellowship and caring groups; and various support groups? Does your congregation have new and recently formed groups such as neighborhood Bible study groups and community outreach programs? Do you have groups based on interest, affinity, age, gender, family, geography, or accountability?

Evaluate your existing groups in light of the four quadrants. In which quadrant would you place each of them? Why? What is the nature of each group? What are their strengths? What warning signs do they show? What signs of growth do they demonstrate? Your questions are certainly not limited to those mentioned above. You may develop your own or use the suggested questions as a starting point. What is necessary is to know where you are at, what your gifts and strengths are, and what elements are missing that might help you grow and move toward your vision.

Accessing

Accessing is preceded by the identification of potential and current small-group leaders and their needs so that they can be provided with the necessary and adequate training and resources. If your congregation has the financial resources, part of equipping your leaders might be sending them to visit different sites that have thriving small-group ministries, in order to expose them to various models of small-group ministry and observe them firsthand, as well as to learn from their experiences and mistakes. You may hold interviews with leaders of small groups in those settings. You may send your staff to attend leadership training and workshops offered by different organizations, whether church related or not. For example, training in small-group communication and dynamics, conflict resolution, problem solving, and decision-making is useful. However, you will need to make the appropriate adaptations to your church situation. Learn and get ideas from others, but do not try to import exactly the same model into your own setting. Your congregation and each small group within your congregation is unique. Use the resource list at the end of this book as you find your own unique ministry. You may form a group of potential small-group leaders and engage them in a study, using this book, as part of their preparation for small-group leadership.

Group coaching or one-on-one mentoring of leaders of small groups is another approach. Jesus did exactly that for his disciples. A similar approach is providing them with hands-on experience in leading small groups—first as an assistant to an experienced leader, then as a leader with the supervision of an experienced leader, and eventually as a leader without supervision. A further step would be to have an assistant for the new leader. By doing that, you will continue to have a pool of new leaders.

A program of continuing education of leaders of small groups will help nurture leaders. Monthly meetings are ideal, but bimonthly or quarterly meetings are also appropriate. However, the longer the intervals, the more difficult it will be to address all the needs of the leaders. The important thing is to plan the learning time with leaders, since training has to be designed and tailored according to the areas identified as needing improvement. During the monthly meeting, you may have a combination of the following, depending on the expressed needs:

1. Worship and praise
2. Prayer and Bible study
3. Curriculum review of the succeeding month
4. Curriculum review of the preceding month
5. Mini-lecture on a topic of choice/need
6. Intercessory prayers/joys and concerns
7. Accountability
8. Fellowship and refreshments
9. Icebreakers and community-building exercises (You may use this time to try out some icebreakers that leaders may use later in their own groups. After going through it, you may discuss the experience and ideas of how it may be adapted to other small-group settings. Ask what worked, what did not, why, and how it can be improved or adapted.)

When it comes to curriculum needs, you may request publishers of religious literature to send you their catalogs, in order to have an idea of what study materials, small-group dynamics resources, and leader training resources are available. Call their customer service department if you have questions. Ask them to describe the particular resource you are interested in. Send for free samples or review copies, if available. Search the Internet under "small-group ministries in churches," "cell churches," or "cell groups" to get ideas from other organizations. Some churches develop and write their own curriculum that is tailored to their unique ministry setting. It is important to keep in mind that as you develop or choose the resources, you need to have a clear focus of providing help for participants as they seek to follow Jesus Christ.

The following are suggested questions for evaluating curriculum resources:

1. How appropriate is the resource to the user group in terms of content, language, illustration, and cultural reference? (It is assumed that you know intimately the nature and needs of your group.) Is the resource age-appropriate? (You may seek the help of professional Christian educators.)
2. Can the resource be adequately covered within the time allotted—for each meeting and for the number of group meetings?
3. How appropriate is this resource for the season within the church year?
4. What kinds of materials are required? Are they easily available? Are they user-friendly without sacrificing content?
5. How appropriate is the resource for this particular group facilitator to use? Does it require training? If so, how much?

6. Is there a leader guide? a student guide?
7. How much preparation time is required? Is it adequate?
8. Does it support the primary task of the church? the mission and vision of the church?
9. How much do training resources cost? Are they affordable?
10. Are there reproducible pages in the leader guide?
11. Does the content reflect the theological position of our church?
12. Is the resource based on Scripture?
13. How does the resource encourage the use of Scripture, tradition, reason, and experience?

Progressing

Progressing refers to growing together in your love for God and for neighbor. In other words, is your group making progress toward your vision for the church? Do you intentionally live out your commitment to love God and love your neighbor? How do you do that on a daily basis? Do you have a system of accountability to ensure that intentional Christian discipleship and nurture happen? Have you experienced transformation in your individual and corporate life? How is that transformation lived out? How have you reached out to others? Have you told others today about the good news of Christ's transforming grace? What testimonies and stories can you tell that speak to the power of God's grace? How have you and others in your group experienced the presence of God in your lives today or this week?

Set aside a time for evaluation at regular intervals. It is not a matter of choosing to do it, but rather when you are going to do it. The quadrants presented in previous chapters can guide the group's self-examination and accountability. Consider writing a covenant that spells out where you want your group to be at the end of the next accountability period. As you define your current reality and recast your vision for the future, you may ask the following questions. Remember, the future may be short-term, such as the next six months, or long-term, such as the next three or four years. It would serve you well to have a combination of short- and long-term visions so that you can measure your progress in small chunks of time while making some movement toward your long-term goal.

1. Where are we today compared with where we were last time?
2. Did we accomplish what we intended to do during this time period?
3. If we did, what can we celebrate?
4. If we did not, why not? What kept us from fulfilling our goal?

5. What can we learn from this experience?
6. How have we created the space for the Holy Spirit to work in and through us?
7. In what ways have we been faithful to the Great Commission and the Great Commandment?
8. Where did we see God's transforming power at work in the lives of people, situations, and settings?
9. How have lives been touched by the love of Jesus?
10. What opportunities did we miss or let pass by? Why?

Recasting

Recasting your vision comes after evaluating your progress. This process is closely linked with the previous step. Recasting is when you make appropriate changes, based on your assessment of your progress and your unique circumstances. Perhaps your vision and goals were unrealistic to start with, or you took an overly radical step that turned off a lot of members or proved too overwhelming or too big too soon. Perhaps it was done in haste without allowing time to listen to the dreams, hopes, and needs of members of your group or faith community. Perhaps the growth and transformation among your members have outpaced your vision. Perhaps members have more time and energy than they had earlier thought. Perhaps the transformation has brought a renewed vigor, enthusiasm, and commitment for the Lord's ministry, so members want to do more for others. In any case, a regular examination of your small-group life in relation to the Great Commandment and the Great Commission will most likely bring about changes toward holiness, peace, and harmony. Regular examination can keep your small group from getting into a rut. Keep challenging yourself to grow and push the edges. You may start with small steps and then continue to take bigger and bolder steps in your faith journey as you continue to gain confidence, experience, and wisdom. As you recast your vision, ask these questions:
1. What is preventing, or could prevent, us from realizing our vision?
2. How can we prepare for those barriers and challenges?
3. What resources (people, information, skills, materials, facilities, money) do we need in order to keep our covenant?
4. How can we access the resources?
5. What areas of group life do we need to learn about, improve, and strengthen?
6. What areas of group life do we need to celebrate and keep doing?

7. How do we measure growth in our relationships within and outside our small group?
8. How do we measure growth in our faith and relationship with God and Jesus Christ?
9. What is our vision for the next accountability period?
10. How are we going to live that out as a group (details of action plan for next period)?

Unless you are specific and intentional about how you are going to live out your life as a small group in relation to the Great Commission and the Great Commandment, you will make hardly any progress toward the realization of your vision. If you do not expect transformation to happen, it never will. If you do not plan to ensure that hospitality, nurture, Christian discipleship, disciple making, faith sharing, Christian community building, teaching and learning, living the Great Commandment and obeying the Great Commission every day, works of justice, compassion, worship, and devotion, they will never happen. That is what casting your vision is all about. That is stewardship. That is accountability, making sure that what you set out to do will actually take place.

This is just the starting point. You have begun your journey. Which direction will you take? Under whose inspiration and guidance will you move? My prayer is that God will give you the wisdom, strength, fortitude, patience, compassion, and humility to empower you and your small-group leaders in your ministry of making disciples of Jesus Christ.

Helpful Resources for Small-Group Ministries

Listed here is a sampling of the available resources related to small-group ministries.

Websites

- The General Board of Discipleship (www.gbod.org)—Includes information about events, reviews, articles, links to other sites, and a wide array of other online resources designed to help leaders of small groups.

- Discipleship Resources (www.discipleshipresources.org)—An online bookstore featuring resources for church leaders, including small groups.

- The Upper Room (www.upperroom.org)—Includes an online bookstore that has resources that can be used with small groups.

- Cokesbury (www.cokesbury.com)—An online bookstore that includes curriculum resources for small groups.

Books

The following books are available from Discipleship Resources. Online bookstore: www.discipleshipresources.org. Phone: 800-685-4370. Fax: 770-442-9742. Address: Discipleship Resources Distribution Center, P.O. Box 1616, Alpharetta, GA 30009-1616.

- *Accountable Discipleship: Living in God's Household,* by Steven W. Manskar.

- *The Christian Small-Group Leader,* by Thomas R. Hawkins.

- *Cultivating Christian Community,* by Thomas R. Hawkins.

- *Guide for Covenant Discipleship Groups,* by Gayle Turner Watson.

- *The Heart's Journey: Christian Spiritual Formation in the Life of a Small Group,* by Barb Nardi Kurtz.

- *Staying Focused: Building Ministry Teams for Christian Formation,* by M. Anne Burnette Hook and Shirley F. Clement.